Practicing Organization Development

**The Change Agent Series
for Groups and Organizations**

MISSION STATEMENT

The books in this series are intended to be cutting-edge, state-of-the-art, innovative approaches to organization change and development. They are written for and by practitioners interested in new approaches to facilitating effective organization change. They are geared to providing both theory and advice on practical applications.

SERIES EDITORS

**William J. Rothwell
Roland Sullivan
Kristine Quade**

EDITORIAL BOARD

**David Bradford
W. Warner Burke
Edith Whitfield Seashore
Robert Tannenbaum
Christopher G. Worley
Shaolin Zhang**

Other Practicing Organization Development Titles

Finding Your Way in the Consulting Jungle: A Guidebook for Organization Development Practitioners
Arthur M. Freedman and Richard E. Zackrison

Facilitating Organization Change: Lessons from Complexity Science
Edwin E. Olson and Glenda H. Eoyang

Appreciative Inquiry: Change at the Speed of Imagination
Jane Magruder Watkins and Bernard J. Mohr

Beyond Change Management: Advanced Strategies for Today's Transformational Leaders
Dean Anderson and Linda Ackerman Anderson

The Change Leader's Roadmap: How to Navigate Your Organization's Transformation
Linda Ackerman Anderson and Dean Anderson

Guiding Change Journeys: A Synergistic Approach to Organization Transformation
Rebecca Chan Allen

Balancing Individual and Organizational Values: Walking the Tightrope to Success
Ken Hultman with Bill Gellermann

The Conscious Consultant: Mastering Change from the Inside Out
Kristine Quade and Renée M. Brown

Organization Development and Consulting: Perspectives and Foundations
Fred Massarik and Marissa Pei-Carpenter

Relationships That Enable Enterprise Change: Leveraging the Client-Consultant Connection
Ron A. Carucci, William A. Pasmore, and the Colleagues of Mercer Delta

Rewiring Organizations for the Networked Economy: Organizing, Managing, and Leading in the Information Age
Stan Herman, Editor

Consulting to Family Businesses: A Practical Guide to Contracting, Assessment, and Implementation
Jane Hilburt-Davis and W. Gibb Dyer, Jr.

The
Innovation
Equation

The Innovation Equation

Building Creativity and Risk Taking in Your Organization

Jacqueline Byrd
Paul Lockwood Brown

JOSSEY-BASS/PFEIFFER
A Wiley Imprint
www.pfeiffer.com

Practicing
Organization
Development

Published by Jossey-Bass/Pfeiffer
A Wiley Imprint
989 Market Street, San Francisco, CA 94103-1741   www.pfeiffer.com

We at Jossey-Bass strive to use the most environmentally sensitive paper stocks available to us. Our publications are printed on acid-free recycled stock whenever possible, and our paper always meets or exceeds minimum GPO and EPA requirements.

Jossey-Bass also publishes its books in a variety of electronic formats. Some content that appears in print may not be available in electronic books.

Acquiring Editor: Josh Blatter
Director of Development: Kathleen Dolan Davies
Developmental Editor: Susan Rachmeler
Editor: Rebecca Taff

Senior Production Editor: Dawn Kilgore
Manufacturing Supervisor: Becky Carreño
Interior and Cover Design: Bruce Lundquist
Illustrations: Richard Sheppard

ISBN: 0-7879-6250-3

Library of Congress Cataloging-in-Publication Data

Byrd, Jacqueline.
The innovation equation: building creativity and risk taking in your organization / Jacqueline Byrd, Paul Lockwood Brown.
     p. cm.—(The practicing organization development series)
Includes bibliographical references and index.
  ISBN 0-7879-6250-3 (alk. paper)
 1. Creative ability in business. 2. Technological
innovations—Management. 3. Risk management. I. Brown, Paul Lockwood,
1961- II. Title. III. Series.
  HD53 .B97 2002
  658.3'14—dc21
2002004069

Printed in the United States of America
Printing   10   9   8   7   6   5   4   3   2   1

Dedication

THIS BOOK IS DEDICATED to the late Dr. Richard E. Byrd, a remarkable innovator and early OD consultant, who said, "Risk taking is the critical mechanism and fundamental skill needed by individuals and organizations to create the accelerated changes and directional shifts necessary to sustain survival, growth, and renewal in business today." These words still ring true, but the time to make them reality is evermore present.

This book is further dedicated to the following Creatrix consultants who took the risk to help bring the innovation equation to life:

Jeanne Bailey	Richard Bents, Ph.D.	Steve Bethke
Thomas Brotski	Renée Brown	Jane Canney
Katherine Curran, Ph.D.	Trina Duncan	Pamela French
Vicki Hargrove, Ph.D.	Susan Harper, Ph.D.	Holly Keller
Barbara Luke	John Mirocha, Ph.D.	Janet Polach, Ph.D.
Kristine Quade	Lou Quast	Ian Stephenson
Eve Stranz	Ipek Uzer	Lorraine Wrafter

Contents

List of Exhibits, Figures, and Tables

Acknowledgments

FIRST, TO THOSE SPECIAL PEOPLE in our lives, Kevin Nickels, my husband, who through his own innovative business actions changed the way I viewed innovation in business. And to my children, Melanie, Christina, and Alison, for the Saturdays and evenings that I couldn't be there. You always seemed to find innovative ways to entertain one another. Thanks. And, finally, to Helen Byrd, whose untimely death spurred creativity and risk taking in her daughter.

And to Colleen Brown, my inspiration, my hope, and my driving force: thank you! For my children, Jacob, Rachel, and Paul, Jr., this is written with the hope that your lives may be more complete.

Also, a special thanks to three people who took their precious time to share their gifts as readers, thinkers, and doers in the field of management and leadership:

William (Bill) Gjetson, Caterpillar Paving Products

William (Bill) Scheurer, University of Minnesota

Terry Schutten, Sacramento County

We offer a special thanks to our editor and friend, Kristine Quade, whose belief that we could offer something to this series even before we believed it inspired us. And thank you to Susan Rachmeler, our developmental editor, for your steadfast review of the book, feedback, and attention to detail. Thank you to Doris Schnable at the Byrd Company for your editorial contributions.

The Innovation Equation

So then she said: What is creativity?
And I responded: To create is to form that
which was not there yesterday, but tomorrow's child.

And then, he said: So what is risk taking?
And I said: To take a risk is something once unspoken,
now spoken—as in the night, we steal away like fairies
on a trip with unknown travelers.

The combination of the two, creativity and risk taking,
explodes that which has not been into the universe.
Innovation is its name!
—J. Byrd

Introduction

WHILE YOU MAY THINK that being creative means being artistic and getting in touch with your inner child and that being a risk taker is all about thrill seeking activities like bungee jumping and/or race car driving, we hope that by writing this book we will influence how you frame these concepts and help you learn how to use them to your advantage in creating innovative applications for yourself, your teams, and your organization. Risk taking coupled with creative ideas is what innovation is about. This book provides an understanding of how to get there.

What's an Innovative Organization?

Let's begin by visualizing an innovative organization. An innovative organization:

- Encourages its members to operate independently;
- Rewards people for being inner-directed and developing their own ideas;
- Values the uniqueness and talents of every contributor;

- Demonstrates resiliency when confronted with setbacks;
- Knows how to thrive in ambiguous circumstances;
- Fosters an environment in which individuals are valued and rewarded for being authentic; and
- Exhibits self-accepting behaviors—"we're good!"

As today's business challenges become increasingly difficult to manage, organizations need innovative solutions to stay competitive. They need to move beyond current business practices to find new ways of doing business that will help ensure future success.

> "There is nothing that is a more certain sign of insanity than to do the same thing over and over and expect the results to be different."
> *Albert Einstein, quoted in* How to Think Like Einstein

A quote from a PricewaterhouseCoopers (2000) study titled, *Innovation and Growth: A Global Perspective,* captures the essence of innovation: "The most valuable organizations of the future will be rich in ideas, embody a culture where innovation is a core capability and value, and will embrace new and unusual ways of fostering innovation. Innovation will be the number one strategic issue for CEOs, as the link between innovation and organizational growth and value creation becomes accepted." The study goes on to say that companies that generate 80 percent of their revenue from new products have typically doubled their market capitalization in a five-year period.

Organizations that actually operate with innovation at their core:

- Respond quickly to changing market requirements;
- Develop new product ideas;
- Increase efficiencies;
- Have a reduced need for working capital;
- Create higher profits; and
- Improve customer service.

We do not advocate creating an organization comprised only of *innovators*, but rather organizations that have *the capacity to be innovative*. There's a subtle but critically important difference here. Innovative capacity can be increased in organizations without expecting each person to be an innovator. Indeed, an organization or team comprised of only innovators usually produces nothing but chaos. Many of the dot.coms of the late 1990s were filled with innovators. However, what some of these companies needed was to temper their organizational profile with people who were good at doing sustaining type work in their organizations. We call these people *sustainers.*

Innovative capacity can be deliberately planned, designed, and built. The keys are (1) fostering creativity and risk taking in employees and (2) creating an environment and culture that supports them. While this is easier said than done, it is necessary in order to create an organization that first values, then creates, and ultimately thrives on innovation. This is a crucial premise set forth in this book: It is indeed possible to foster innovation.

Our Commitment to You, the Reader

In this book, we show you how to create and support the development of innovative ideas in organizations. You'll learn how to set an innovative *aim*; how to *assess* innovative strengths of each contributor; how to *activate* the seven creativity and risk-taking drivers that impact capacity to innovate; and how to *apply* all of this to get the kind of results you previously only dreamed were possible. We know what drives innovation, and we know how to bring it to life in organizations and with the teams and individuals who comprise the organization.

As you read this book, you will:

- Gain a greater appreciation and understanding of the value of innovation and its significance in fostering an organization's or team's continual growth and development;

- Understand the relationship between creativity, risk taking, and innovation and translate and leverage that understanding to accelerate your innovative capacity;

- Acquire insight into your own and the organization's or team's current levels of creativity and risk taking and learn how that affects innovative capacity;

- Understand the drivers of creativity and risk taking and how these drivers can be effectively used to accelerate innovative capacity in organizations, teams, and individuals; and

- Apply the drivers of creativity and risk taking to a specific aim of the organization/team, that is, learn how to be innovative with a clear purpose.

In the journey to discover how to make organizations, teams, and ourselves more innovative, we've found that it is only possible by understanding the power of creativity and risk taking. These two things make it possible for us to uniquely contribute to the world and those around us. This combination in furthering ideas, creating possibilities, and ultimately innovating is the foundation of the innovation equation.

Organization of this Book

Chapter 1 provides a framework for shaping your perspective on innovation. In this chapter, we lay the foundation of our thinking and expose the reader to some other common schools of thought. We examine the nature of innovation and its constructs and detail some of the current thinking on innovation.

In the second chapter, we introduce the key elements of innovation: creativity and risk taking. We explore the nature of creativity and risk taking in organizational life and link them to their impact on innovation. Readers are introduced to a questionnaire that measures creativity and risk taking, which together create innovation. The results of the questionnaire are plotted on a matrix (the Creatrix), which includes eight possible orientations. Each of the eight orientations is described in detail, including useful information on the value and contributions of each orientation.

In the third chapter, we discuss what drives creativity and risk taking. The seven drivers are introduced, and we examine the nature of each in detail.

Chapter 4 introduces the reader to two tales of innovation. The first is one of the Grimms' fairy tales and the second is a contemporary version from our own innovative imaginations. Each tale highlights the seven drivers of creativity and risk taking. Illustrating these concepts in story form is our unique way of bringing the seven drivers to life.

In Chapter 5, we talk about inhibiting factors—the stop signs to innovation. Here we examine how organizations, teams, and individuals inadvertently quell innovative efforts. This awareness helps us understand how to apply the innovation equation. Further, we introduce a series of challenges that can help to overcome these stop signs.

In the sixth chapter, we discuss how to apply the innovation equation. We detail each of the four A's: *aim, assess, activate,* and *apply.* This step-by-step approach to innovation is an effective means for increasing innovative capacity in organizations, teams, and individuals. Included are three in-depth case studies on how to build innovative teams, followed by an invitation to the reader to translate this to his or her organization.

Chapters 7 and 8 focus on the individual—both as an innovative leader and as an innovative consultant, respectively. Four key strategies for becoming an innovative leader are detailed in Chapter 7, while Chapter 8 deals with creativity and risk taking from the perspective of the practitioner.

Finally, we have included Appendixes containing our nationally recognized creativity and risk-taking simulation as well as a process for creating innovative ideas in teams.

Now turn the page and start learning how to bring innovation to life in your organizations and teams.

Ideas for the Consultant

If working with teams or setting the stage for working with an entire organization, consider the following:

- Have the members of the team visualize an innovative organization.

- Have them describe the characteristics of an innovative organization or team. Ask them to expound on the themes and lay out the reasons why they consider their example to be an innovative organization.

1

Perspectives on Innovation

The Nature of Innovation in Organizations

According to the *American Heritage Dictionary* (1994), "Innovation is the *act* of introducing something new." Notice that the definition doesn't say something that has never existed before, implying that a modification of a current product is not an innovation. Nor does it say that every idea is innovative. Note the words, *act of introducing* (risk taking), and the word *new* (creative). These concepts, creativity and risk taking, in combination, are what innovation is all about.

Innovation = Creativity × Risk Taking

Innovation manifests itself in myriad ways, small and large, every day. The invention of the fax machine was an innovative act. So was being the first restaurant owner to put out a fish bowl to collect people's business cards. In exchange for a few free lunches, this innovative person was able to discover where his or her lunch crowd was coming from.

Further, innovation does not have to be dramatic or large scale in nature. Incremental improvements are indeed incremental innovations. They add great value to the success of a company. For example, changing the size or color of Post-it® Notes has provided additional business opportunities for 3M. Certainly one wouldn't want to rely solely on these types of incremental innovative solutions for continued business success, but their value remains nonetheless.

Innovation keeps companies alive through continuous renewal and growth. Without innovative ideas, a company stagnates and may even cease as a going concern. Thus innovation becomes a must, rather than an option. Organizational innovation may range from introducing new products and services to complete reinvention of the organization.

Innovation may mean greater product differentiation or diversification. For example, Pepsi-Cola now has Pepsi, Diet Pepsi, Pepsi One, Diet Pepsi Twist, and so on and so on. Tobacco companies, albeit slow to recognize their ultimate fate, have begun to diversify their product lines to include food and other consumables. Ultimately, this may include redefining paradigms of their core business. For example, if railroads had shifted their paradigm to define their core business as the transportation industry rather than the railroad business, perhaps we'd be flying on Northern Pacific Airways rather than Northwest Airlines.

In other words, you will be left behind if you don't innovate. Take a moment to reflect on the recent history of your organization. Would you characterize it as more competitive as a result of its innovative efforts? Maybe it hasn't been innovative at all and as a result is declining in market share, profitability, or some other measure of success. While the challenges may seem daunting, it's not too late to make adjustments. That's the beauty of building your innovative capacity: it creates the capacity for change, which can help companies modify, adapt, survive, and even thrive in these competitive times.

Consider the following perspectives. Leonard (1998) states, "Innovation, the source of sustained advantage of most companies, depends upon the individual and collective expertise of employees." Hirshberg (1998) says, "Innovation requires the capacity to disdain tradition and break with comfortable routines and mastered skills." Drucker (1985) defines innovation as "the effort to create purposeful, focused change in an enterprise's economic or social potential."

These definitions require breaking with the status quo and, rather than focusing on the past, they focus on future possibilities. Organizations have long recognized the need for innovation. In fact, 3M built its reputation on innovation and is headquartered on Innovation Boulevard! However, the question of how to become more innovative remains a mystery to most. Some look to other companies to benchmark innovative strategies. Others articulate the need in a vision or mission that's supposed to foster innovation. Still others seek prescriptive, proven formulas, not realizing that such plans run counter to what fosters innovation.

The Necessity of Organizational Innovation

Is the wise old adage "necessity is the mother of invention" applicable today? Can we really afford to wait until the need proves great before we're forced to innovate a solution? In today's competitive marketplace, playing the waiting game is a telltale sign that your organization doesn't understand just how much risk it's taking by failing to act. To be anything less than proactive when it comes to building innovation in your organization is simply giving the upper hand to your competitors.

Most of us value the results of innovative ideas. Innovative ideas usually make our lives easier. Telephones, electric lights, freeways, automobiles, digital phones, airplanes, skyscrapers, colored pencils, calculators, clocks, computers, refrigerators, tape dispensers, and blenders were all once original ideas and innovative responses to challenges.

If we think about the obstacles and constraints our organizations and teams are facing, we'll find that at times the solutions to these issues require us to introduce new ways or means of doing things, that is, a creative solution that someone or some group took the risk to introduce. As today's business challenges are becoming increasingly difficult to manage, today's organizations have to develop innovative solutions to stay competitive. The viability and success of an organization may very well depend on your personal and your team's capacity to foster this capability.

Often when we're confronted with a challenging business obstacle, we merely hope someone will come up with a good idea or strategy—after all, isn't that the way it's worked in the past? Sometimes we may even sit back and criticize those in charge for proposing half-baked solutions. Indeed, if the solution is half-baked, how come it doesn't include the critical insights from those (like you or me) who obviously know a better way? Specifically, why don't we take the risk to introduce our perspectives or come up with new solutions?

Breakthrough innovations are often serendipitous in nature. The value of strategic planning notwithstanding, organizational breakthroughs are frequently the function of an epiphany, a sudden intuitive realization. All of us have epiphanies. Many times they occur after we have separated ourselves from the immediate issues at hand. For example, taking a break from wrestling with difficult issues around the conference table to exercise over lunch has lead to more than one epiphany. Whether we're working out, waiting for an airplane, or driving home, breakthrough thinking happens at unusual times. It is often unplanned. Limiting breakthrough thinking to brainstorming sessions in the boardroom is an almost certain prescription for failure.

A Limiting Mentality: Organizational Messages That Inhibit Innovation

Organizations, teams, and individuals have trouble with innovating because they often have an arrogance, frequently exhibited as complacency, about their past success; further, they cling to the comfort of predictability and conformity. Ideas outside the realm of current paradigms are criticized as not reflecting the core values of the organization. Other times our immediate supervisor has opportunity areas, and we can't forget the "What's in it for me?" attitude that seems to prevail in such circumstances. The reality is all these things and more contribute to inhibiting innovation.

Landrum (1993) states that large organizations stifle innovators because of the following:

- Arrogance,
- Short-term mentality,
- Expert syndrome,
- MBA syndrome,
- Cultural dysfunction,
- Intolerance of mavericks,
- Risk adversity,
- Micro versus macro vision,
- Not invented here syndrome, and
- A Wall Street mentality.*

Albeit unintentional, these phenomena suggest powerful forces are at work in many of today's large organizations. This mentality provides opportunities for smaller, less established firms that operate with higher degrees of innovative capacity to take advantage. Innovative companies know they have limitations. They look

---

*From Gene N. Landrum, *Profiles of Genius*, (Amherst, NY: Prometheus Books). Copyright © Gene N. Landrum. Reprinted by permission of the publisher.

for opportunities beyond their immediate realms, depend on everyone to contribute, celebrate the mavericks within their ranks, take greater risks, and establish visions of the future that allow for potentially disparate realities. They develop and maintain a sense of urgency with respect to virtually everything they do.

In *Creative Destruction*, Foster and Kaplan (2001) say:

> "Corporate control systems also undermine the ability of the organization to innovate at the pace and scale of the market. Under the assumption of continuity, for example, the arguments for building a new business can be turned back since its probable success cannot be proven in advance. Corporate control systems limit creativity through their dependence on convergent thinking. Convergent thinking focuses on clear problems and provides well-known solutions quickly. It thrives on focus."

Innovation does not depend on convergent thinking. Innovation depends on divergent thinking, on the ability to change and move in directions that are nonlinear. In Edward De Bono's words, it depends on lateral thinking. In *Lateral Thinking: Creativity Step by Step*, de Bono (1973) says:

> "Lateral thinking is quite distinct from vertical thinking, which is the traditional type of thinking. In vertical thinking one moves forward by sequential steps each of which must be justified. The distinction between the two sorts of thinking is sharp. For instance, in lateral thinking one uses information not for its own sake but for its effect. In lateral thinking one may have to be wrong at some stage in order to achieve a correct solution; in vertical thinking (logic or mathematics) this would be impossible. In lateral thinking one may deliberately seek out irrelevant information; in vertical thinking one selects out only what is relevant."

Corporate directors and shareholders' continued pressure to improve organizational financial performance often requires more than linear improvements; they require breakthrough innovations. According to Hamel and Prahalad (1994), "Most companies long ago reached the point of diminishing returns in their incremental improvement programs."

The key is to understand what fosters innovation within an organization. Little happens without the understanding that creativity and risk taking are the essential components of innovation. Appropriate risk taking coupled with creative ideas is what innovation is all about. Organizations that want greater creativity, risk taking, and innovation must realize that this requires paradigm shifts. Shifts in thinking that, until they become well-rooted, may be inadvertently undermined by their own actions. The risk is not in undertaking the endeavor; the risk is in failing to remove obstacles impeding success, obstacles that include management's own actions. As organizations demand greater creativity and innovation from their members, they must provide the environments that encourage the behaviors they desire. Failing to do so is tantamount to spinning your wheels; all talk, with no action.

Creativity and Innovation

Think back for a minute to the definition we presented at the beginning of this chapter: Innovation is the act of introducing something new. The *something new* has its origins in creativity. Innovation demands creativity. Foster and Kaplan (2001) say, "The underlying element in all innovation is creativity. Only by understanding creativity can one grapple with what is needed for sustained performance."

Creativity is the ability to develop new ideas. Those ideas may be as mundane as turning eggshells into little faces or as sublime as the great pyramids of Egypt. They may be as practical as the saltshaker or as absurd as a Pig-Latin alphabet. Regardless of scope, creativity is synonymous with new ideas (Byrd, 1974).

Restrictions on experimenting with new ideas are imposed on most people from early childhood. Children are instructed to keep within the black lines of the coloring book, and doodling is often discouraged and viewed as unproductive. Creating fanciful stories is often interpreted as lying, and pretending is tolerated only until a child reaches a certain age—then it becomes embarrassing. Being out of line—be it the line to the cafeteria, the washroom, the water fountain, or the playground—is considered bad behavior.

Adults on the job are also caught in a variety of binds. Management often seeks coordination, implementation, and follow-through, squeezing any room for creativity out of the equation. Often creativity threatens the status quo. After all, organizations need systems, and what good are systems if people deviate from them? We're not advocating greater creativity in all situations or creativity for its own sake. For example, do we want our heart surgeon or pilot to get creative on us?

Actually we might. If that surgeon or pilot is faced with a situation that demands creativity in order to save our life, we don't want them to necessarily follow the book. Similarly, when our organization or team is confronted with an obstacle that needs to be overcome, we need creativity—and lots of it! Like anything else, knowing when, where, and how much is crucial.

Creativity is measured by originality. In fact, originality is the most commonly acknowledged facet of creativity (Bailin, 1992; Runco & Okuda, 1988). And all of us are original to some degree. But let's not confuse originality with intelligence. People often assume that originality and intelligence are correlated. There is little evidence to support this assumption. Many people with only average intelligence have many original ideas, and some of the brightest people seldom have original thoughts.

So is there a single best definition of creativity? We asked a number of people to provide some definitions. What follows is a partial list of what we heard:

1. Quality of thinking that inspires ingenuity and imagination;
2. Producing something useful that establishes worth/enjoyment and that has not been done before;
3. Expressing yourself openly;
4. Putting things together in a new way;
5. Conjuring something unique;
6. God;
7. Like . . . your imagination, but in a different way;
8. A different way of looking at things;
9. Coming up with new ways of doing things;
10. Looking to do or create something without being hindered by past rules or perceived boundaries;
11. Stretching till it hurts and feels good all at the same time;
12. Doing something and having fun by doing it;
13. Ability, skill, talent that enables one to be free to envision something new or better;
14. The truly great artist has the eyes of a child and vision of a sage (Pablo Cassals);
15. Be not afraid of where your next idea will lead (Charles Eames);
16. Deep within the heart we find the creative self (Cappacchione);
17. Using new or existing ideas to get results in a different way than one would normally think of;
18. Using all outlets available;

19. Being able to build off of old theories or ideas to make new theories;

20. Letting imagination flow independently—no restrictions; and

21. The raw materials for innovation.

Given that creativity is characterized by originality, expressiveness, and imagination (*American Heritage Dictionary*, 1994), it would seem to follow that there isn't one single best definition that works for everyone.

How then do we make these definitions, or any other for that matter, come alive in a shared way in our organizations? Most people within organizations will tell you how much they value creativity. However, as we discussed earlier, creativity in organizations is often suppressed much more often than it is supported. This isn't because mangers have a vendetta against creativity. Everyday creativity is undermined unintentionally in work environments that were established—for entirely good reasons—to maximize business imperatives such as coordination, productivity, and systems control. Unfortunately, the unintended consequence of maintaining the status quo is muted creativity. Only when we focus on how to foster and nurture creativity in others, our organizations, and ourselves will innovation occur.

Fostering Creativity in Organizations

One of the most wonderful things organizations have going for them is that people already have an intrinsic desire to go beyond—to learn, to grow, and to aspire to possibilities within themselves; albeit to varying degrees, we all have this motivation—to use more of ourselves, to tap into our creative capacities.

By understanding this important premise, organizations and individuals can reap the innovative rewards. Much of the work of Rogers (1961), Maslow (1962), Tillich (1957), Riesman (1950), and Fromm (1947) provides a foundation for understanding this drive to hear our own voice. "It's the voice of our true selves which summons us back to live productively, develop fully and harmoniously—that is to become what we potentially are" (Fromm, 1947).

Robert Fritz (1991) talks about this voice and specifically addresses it to creativity:

"Let's face it, most of us have the suspicion that there is much more to life than what we have been led to expect. Our lives are filled with secret possibilities—possibilities that there are dimensions to our selves, depths of our being, and heights to our aspirations that are lurking just below the surface. Despite years of attempts by relatives, friends, acquaintances, and society to bring us to our senses, the desire and impulse to reach for that which is highest in us is still there. After all the appeals to reason, we still have the very human urge to do something that matters to us. Despite all the times that society has endeavored to kill that instinct in us, it just won't die."

One of the most wonderful things about human beings is this desire we have to develop into something more than we currently are. We only use small portions of our brain and creative potential. This creative capacity enables every individual organism the opportunity to continually re-create itself; re-creations that ultimately lead to our self-actualization.

"The self-actualized person believes the locus of evaluation lies within himself. Less and less does he look back to others for approval or disapproval. The only question that really matters to him is, 'Am I living in a way which is deeply satisfying to me, and which truly expresses me?'" (Rogers, 1961). Like a blade of grass growing beneath the cement, we all have a need to let ourselves out of constraining spaces, seeking to find the crack that will lead to sunshine and growth.

"Humans have a natural drive to explore and create, a drive that derives from an urge as basic as hunger or sex" (Robinson & Stern, 1998). This basic primal instinct is the reason we often react so strongly when people reject our ideas. Our creations are the gifts of our selves to the world. Our creative contributions may range from a special cookie recipe to engineering work that helps put people on the moon. Regardless of size or scope, there is an inherent value in each of our creative contributions.

Motivating for Greater Creativity

Knowing we all have creative potential is not enough. We know its value, but it will sit dormant unless we stimulate it. The question is: What will we do to tap into it, to foster it in our organizations, our teams, and ourselves? This is where the gift of motivation becomes so important. Teresa Amabile (2001) says, "According to the intrinsic motivation principle of creativity, people will be most creative when they are motivated primarily by the interest, enjoyment, satisfaction, and challenge of the work itself (intrinsic motivators)."

Self-motivated creativity is uniquely individual in nature; further, the will to create is a powerful force at both the individual and organizational levels. Highly motivated and creative organizations tend to outperform organizations that may have other significant compelling factors, such as greater resources, clearer goals, or more efficient operations. Motivation is about pushing and striving forward. Consider the following list of individuals: Albert Einstein, Susan B. Anthony, Virginia Woolf, Walt Disney, and Lee Iacocca, and these organizations: Microsoft, 3M, NASA, and McDonald's. What do they all have in common? Not only did they recognize and incorporate creativity as a value, but they acted on their intrinsic motivation to become more—each ultimately contributing to society in profound ways. While these are high-profile examples, keep in mind that most innovations are the result of ordinary people and organizations seizing both ordinary and extraordinary opportunities.

Therefore, as we think about how motivation impacts creative efforts, it is important to understand its purpose. It is not motivation for production or motivation for financial reward. While noble pursuits, these will ultimately fall short in terms of innovation. Intrinsic motivation arises when individuals feel both self-determined and competent in their work (Deci & Ryan, 1985). Self-determined, competent people do not thrive in smothering organizations. This premise has its origins in Herzberg's (1966) motivator-hygiene theory, which has two components: maintenance factors, which are necessary to maintain a desired level of employee satisfaction, and motivational factors, such as recognition, responsibility, and growth potential. These motivational factors, such as potential for growth, profoundly impact an individual's willingness to contribute through creation.

Additionally, in *How to Kill Creativity*, Amabile (1998) offers this helpful perspective:

> "Specifically, managers will need to understand that creativity has three parts: expertise, the ability to think flexibly and imaginatively, and motivation. Managers can influence the first two, but doing so is costly and slow. It would be far more effective to increase employees' intrinsic motivation and as a result reaping the rewards of their creativity."

Thus it becomes important for organizations to create environments that allow for greater intrinsic motivation. These environments in turn foster creativity and thus help create opportunities for building innovative capacity.

Risk Taking and Innovation

The second component of innovation is risk taking. Recall again the definition of innovation: The act of introducing something new. Taking risks is the only way that creative ideas become reality. Risk is a deliberately willed activity that creates and accelerates change.

Risk taking means that a person is willing to push his or her ideas forward at some potential risk to his or her own security, career, reputation, or self-esteem. It is acting in the face of potential loss to realize potential benefits (Byrd, 1974). *Risk taking is the ability to drive new ideas forward in the face of adversity.*

Risk taking is simply the difference between your reach and your grasp (Gelb, 1998). Risk taking is not an inborn trait. That is, you are not born a high or low risk taker. Some psychologists believe that human beings have an inborn tendency for creativity, growth, and self-actualization (Roweton, 1989). This is what we believe. Others have argued that human personality is adjustable enough for one to become a dependent, risk-avoiding, passive sycophant who cannot be reactive and is helpless in dealing with the environment (Agor, 1991; Winslow, 1990). In other words, there is an innate resistance to take risks beyond what's acceptable in their immediate environment.

> "Every definition I read (about risk) was depressing, packed with words like danger, hazard, peril, and exposure, chance of injury, damage, and loss. It's not surprising your life is worth a noble motive—it became clear to me why risk taking makes us so anxious. After all, haven't we heard all our lives that we should avoid dangerous hazards and perils?"
>
> *Walter Anderson*, The Greatest Risk of All

Many of us work with people who are afraid to take risks; as a result they become paralyzed to inaction. There is so much wasted potential because of letting fear drive our choices. Later on in life, we often hear people say that they've been shortchanged. In reality, they've shortchanged themselves because risk-taking opportunities are everywhere; they simply chose not to take action. We also see lots of organizations that miss critical market opportunities. Consequently, they miss the chance to become more. They were afraid to take a risk and fail and failed anyhow. These are the challenges that we face every day. Rarely do we find ourselves with all the data to make a 100 percent correct decision. And if we do find ourselves in that situation, well, we've mitigated all of the risk out of the equation. Understanding risk taking is such a critical component to our success that any person or company failing to realize this jeopardizes its own well-being through ignorance.

But taking risks just to take risks is pointless. You must be able to see a positive payoff in taking the risks. People who take risks just for the sake of taking risks are addicted to the thrill, not to the appropriateness of the risk given the situation and the potential loss and gains.

Framing a New View of Risk Taking

Rather then play to our natural fears associated with extreme risk-taking behavior, our goal is to frame a new understanding of risk taking.

What's a risk to one person may not be a risk to another. People, teams, and organizations all develop fairly predictable patterns of risk taking. When we determine and become aware of our risk-taking propensities, we can begin to predict our responses to different situations (problem solving, conflict resolution, idea generation, and so forth). This knowledge permits better risk management.

We asked a number of people to define risk taking, just as we did with creativity. Here is a sample of what some of them said:

1. Investment of effort and/or resources with the intention of potential gains, while understanding the possibility of zero return;

2. Betting on the come—establish the bang for the buck;

3. Going out on a limb;

4. Taking a chance;

5. Doing something outside the box;

6. Trying something new without knowing whether it is right or not;

7. Anything without a sure outcome;

8. Doing something that's not a sure success, but one in which the odds are appropriate to the potential value;

9. Making a choice that has the possibility of undesirable results;

10. Doing something I haven't done before;

11. Taking action without penalty of failure;

12. Dangerous fun in the unknown;

13. Pursuing an idea despite the possibility that it could be unsuccessful;

14. Individual risk should be proportionate to the level of return;

15. Ability to move beyond a comfort zone;

16. To envision and implement change that may have ramifications to taking action. In order to thrive and survive, the organization must value and reward risk taking;

17. Cultivating the dream and then setting the intention; and

18. Believing in the beauty of your dream.

Regardless of the definition, there is within our human spirit the desire to take more risks. It is a part of our human makeup.

"Most of us have, or know someone who has, shared the sadness of not having taken a risk to live somewhere else, change jobs, or share more love with their parents, children, or significant other. Over the years, whenever I asked older adults what, if any, regrets they had, one theme emerged loud and clear: Looking back they wished they had taken more risks to be themselves. The ability to take action, to actually risk something, is something we don't always do. However, the sadness we feel as a result of not taking risks is a clear indication that it is part of the human spirit. It is linked to motivation. A part that, when wasted, cannot often be recovered." (Leider, 1999)

Becoming more willing to take risks is not easy. Change requires a willingness to accept criticism and to withstand frustration and even condemnation. It means developing authenticity, resiliency, and a self-accepting attitude. But taking risks makes us feel successful. If you aren't motivated to take more risks in your life, you're likely to remain where you are and regret those things that you never did. Consider the following risks:

- Asking for a raise or promotion;

- Enrolling in a class;

- Undertaking a new project;

- Speaking your mind in a meeting;

- Confronting sacred cows; and

- Public speaking or leading a meeting.

Which ones have you taken lately, if any? Which ones make you feel anxious? Which inspires the most fear in you? All of these have an element of risk. None is life-threatening. Yet they may conjure fear and even avoidance in some of us. When they are undertaken, afterward we often feel more alive and successful, primarily because deep down we believe in ourselves. Certainly one learns liberating endeavors encourage nonlinear behavior. That is, success begets success in new untold ways. When we don't take risks, we are afraid to bet on ourselves, even if we believe that we're capable of doing more. Daniel Bursting, quoted in Daniel Kehrer's (1989) *Doing Business Boldly*, writes, "Historically, risk takers are people who shatter the illusion of knowledge. They are willing to try something that everyone thinks is outrageous or stupid."

Fostering Risk Taking in Organizations

There are many organizations that miss critical market or other paradigm shifts and miss opportunities because they didn't have all the information to make a decision—companies that wait until all the cows come home. By then, the competition is already out ahead. Rarely will we have all of the information and if we do, there is not much risk. We have to take risks for the success of our organizations . . . and for ourselves.

Ask most people within an organization and they will tell you that they want to contribute to the success of the organization. Yet organizations don't know how to capitalize on or leverage this reality. In a study of seven hundred managers, Shapira (1995) found the following perceptions and practices regarding risk taking:

- Managers referred primarily to the downside of risk and

- They attended more to the negative or possible loss than to the probability of success.

In this study we see strong evidence that managers view risk taking as threatening. They tend to focus on the downside of risk. By concentrating on the negatives or potential losses, they quell attempts to succeed. Further, they rely on their own perceptions in discerning threats associated with risk. We seek far too much perfection and predictability to take the necessary risks in our organizations or our selves. The interesting thing is that from earliest times human beings have been risk takers. As a species, how would we have survived if we hadn't been creative and taken risks with the wide variety of animals and threats that surrounded our primitive ancestors? Thorpe (2000) remarks, "Slow, soft humans are the last creatures one would expect to survive in this wilderness of our world. However, we not only survived, but also actually thrived because of our ability to take risks and break the rules, changing strategies in seconds, rather than generations." Although we now live in a wildly different world from those primitive cultures, the truth in this sentiment remains today.

Challenge yourself, for a moment, to think about what risk taking brings to an organization. Risk taking enables growth. Growth comes when we have the courage to lose sight of the shore and travel in unchartered waters. To be sure, peril is often close at hand; but without risk, there is no reward. As organizations grow, however, they often quit taking the risks that they used to take to get them where they are today. Stability and consistency become more important than new ideas and going head-to-head with the competition. In *Highwire Management*, Calvert (1993) says:

> "If you want to be an average manager or have an average organization, little risk taking is required. But, if you're set on high gains, then it demands that you walk on the highwire of management risks. Risk is like walking on a thick tightrope high above the ground without a safety net."

Kouzes and Posner (1987) emphasize that learning from the successes and failures that result from risk taking is "a key that unlocks the door" to opportunity in business. They identify the "hardiness factor" as a requisite for mastering risk. Individuals can keep trying despite failures and focus on the learning rather than on the outcome. In the language of Kouzes and Posner, organizations can foster hardiness by:

- Offering more rewards than punishments;
- Choosing tasks that are challenging, but within the person's skill level to build a sense of control; and
- Encouraging people to see change as full of possibilities and to build an attitude of change.

This hardiness is nothing more than increasing our risk-taking tolerance, a tolerance that if unattended will dwindle over time, resulting in our favoring an attitude of conservatism rather than change.

Hirshberg (1998) writes, "Every business needs to develop strategies to overcome fear, discomfort, and resistance. Fostering a corporate culture that accommodates opposing viewpoints without negative repercussions is a good starting point, but even this is not easy." Developing an authentic culture is a daunting task that requires commitment, time, and energy. It requires shifting conventional thinking to embrace, rather than shy away from risk. It means taking risk-management concepts, reframing them to include positive attributes, and encouraging healthy aspects of risk taking into all aspects of the organization.

In one sense, healthy risk taking can be viewed as experimentation. Thomke (2001) writes, " Experimentation lies at the heart of every company's ability to innovate. In other words, the systematic testing of ideas is what enables companies to create and refine their products. In fact, no product can be a product without having first been an idea that was shaped, to one degree or another through the process of experimentation" [taking risks]. Here we begin to see yet another perspective on the value and nature of risk taking to organizations. And within the definition of experimentation there are also different tolerances, ranging from conservative laboratory analysis to bold entrepreneurial type approaches of betting on the come.

Innovation = Creativity x Risk Taking

We've made some important discoveries in our work to date. Foremost is the belief that innovation is synonymous with creativity. Our point of view is that creativity is an integral part of innovation, but it is not innovation in itself. Innovation is also about risk taking.

We also believe that measuring the innovative capabilities of organizations is not something that's being done. This is due primarily to the fact that people believe it can't be clearly measured and defined—that it's too elusive and complex to measure. But over time each of us, and even our organizations, develop a unique and unmistakable creative and risk-taking orientation. This orientation (high, moderate, or low) may change during different periods of our life or the life cycle of our organization, but each person's and organization's current creative and risk-taking orientation can be measured. We will explore this in the next chapter.

In addition, many people try to explain innovation by reporting on retrospective case studies that describe successful innovative applications in organizations. That is, they write about the characteristics of innovation in organizations that have proven to be innovative. Retrospective studies of specific organizations capture only one point in time; they don't help with the future.

Further, innovation is often characterized as needing to be dramatic or radical if it's to have any benefit. Not only is this untrue, but it perpetuates the belief that innovation is beyond the capabilities of each and every person in the organization, thus discouraging attempts by would-be innovators.

Let's think about the big picture for a moment. The willingness to take risks and drive creative ideas to fruition has resulted in the many valuable products we use today. We might still be cooking over an open fire, storing food in the earth, and using horses as our primary means of transportation had certain people not taken the risks to push their creative ideas. Indeed, we wouldn't have fax machines, cell phones, or personal computers if it weren't for those people who were willing to be creative and take risks. Throughout time, creative people and risk takers have been instrumental in making our lives easier and more interesting.

These are the true innovators, aren't they? Are these people so unusual? Are they so different from you and me and the organizations we all work for? No, they are like us. We are not seeking to create organizations of *innovators*, but rather organizations that have *the capacity to be innovative.* The difference between the two will unfold as we continue our discussion. For now, we ask you to accept the fact that innovative capacity can be increased in individuals and organizations.

In this book we take the concept of innovation and make it real in terms of understanding what it is, how it can be applied, and how individuals, teams, and organizations can accelerate their innovative capacities.

Ideas for the Consultant

If working with teams or setting the stage for work with an entire organization:

- Break the definition of innovation into two parts. Remember, innovation is the act (risk taking) of introducing something new (creativity). Explore each aspect of the equation. (We are intentionally leaving out how you do this so that you can innovate your own new creative approach to exploring these concepts.)

- Ask them to consider the following:

  Does the act of innovation always produce something better?

  Is breakthrough innovation always necessary?

  What are examples of incremental innovations? (And breakthrough innovations?)

- Assert the thesis that we all can be more creative and take more risks. Discuss it. Where does the discussion go? Toward an unlimited future of possibilities? Or somewhere else? Why?

- Have people discuss self-actualization. How does it fit with the *Innovation Equation's* premise that we all can be more creative and take more risks?

- What makes it hard to take risks? Take the opportunity to explore where the messages around risk taking and creativity come from.

- Brainstorm two ideas for increasing creativity in ourselves or others.

- Brainstorm two ideas for greater risk taking in ourselves or others.

(2)

Assessing
Innovative Capacity

BY NOW OUR THESIS IS CLEAR: Innovation is a function of creativity and risk taking.

$$Innovation = Creativity \times Risk\ Taking$$

But so what if we know that innovation is a function of creativity and risk taking? What added value does that have in helping us build innovative capacity in teams, organizations, or ourselves? It doesn't, unless it can be measured and the results can translate into value. The value provided is in being able to build the innovative capacity of organizations, teams, and individuals to enable them to start contributing innovative ideas, services, or products.

If we are able to measure people's capacity to be creative and take risks, we can characterize their current innovative capacity. That is, their capability of producing innovative ideas, services, or products. Measuring innovative capacity will help you understand what particular types of ideas, products, or services are capable of being generated. Further, it provides a framework for understanding creativity and risk taking in terms that make them desirable, rather than something to be managed or avoided at all costs. The Innovation-X Questionnaire was developed in order to measure these dimensions.

The Assessment

Assessment instruments, especially self-assessments, have been used for many years in a variety of ways. Some of the more powerful self-assessments include the Myers-Briggs Type Indicator (MBTI), FIRO-B, and the Strong Interest Inventory. These instruments have proven to be reliable, but it is up to the individual taking the instrument to be honest with himself or herself in order to obtain accurate measurements. We urge you to be honest when taking the Innovation-X Questionnaire (X marks the spot of the intersection between creativity and risk taking).

An implicit assumption of the Innovation-X Questionnaire is that, over a lifetime, people develop a general predisposition toward creativity and risk taking (Byrd, 1986, 2000). The scales were constructed with the assumption that individuals will take the inventory when things are "going well" for them. Although it is possible for a recent traumatic incident in a respondent's life to impact the way he or she scores, the norms are accurate for interpretive purposes. When taking the inventory, don't think too much about the questions or answers. Remember, there are no right or wrong answers—simply different preferences. Go with your first intuition; it's usually the most accurate. The assessment (see Exhibit 2.1) should take no more than five minutes to complete.

Exhibit 2.1. Innovation-X Questionnaire

	Strongly Disagree		Somewhat Disagree			Somewhat Agree		Strongly Agree	
	1	2	3	4	5	6	7	8	9
1 I feel free not to do what others expect of me.									
2 There are a variety of solutions to every problem.									
3 I will risk a friendship in order to say or do what I believe is necessary.									
4 Inventors contribute more than political leaders do.									
5 I feel free to show both friendly and unfriendly feelings to strangers.									
6 Daydreaming is a useful activity.									
7 New situations do not frighten me.									
8 I often fantasize about things I'd like to do.									
9 I can cope with the ups and downs of life.									
10 What others consider chaos does not bother me.									

After you have answered each question, add the numerical value of the responses under each of the headings for the *odd*-numbered questions. Divide this number by five. That is, (1) ___ + (3) ___ + (5) ___ + (7) ___ + (9) ___ = ___ /5 = ___. This is your risk-taking score.

Next, do the same for the even-numbered questions, like this: (2) ___ + (4) ___ + (6) ___ + (8) ___ + (10) ___ = ___ /5 = ___. This is your creativity score.

Now, plot these scores on the Creatrix grid, as shown in the example in Figure 2.1. In this example, the person had a calculated risk-taking score of 8 and a calculated creativity score of 6. She plotted herself on the Creatrix and learned that she is a Practicalizer.

Figure 2.1. Sample Innovation Orientation on the Creatrix

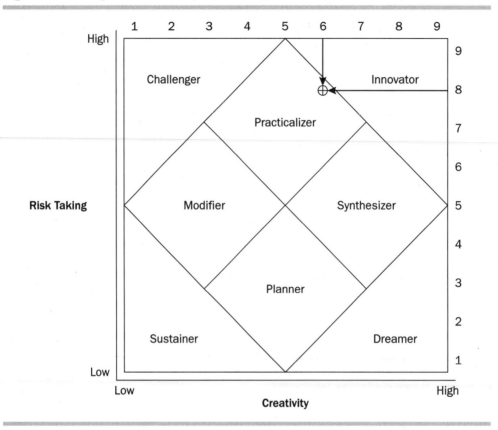

Plot your own calculated scores on the grid in Figure 2.2.

Figure 2.2. Your Innovation Orientation

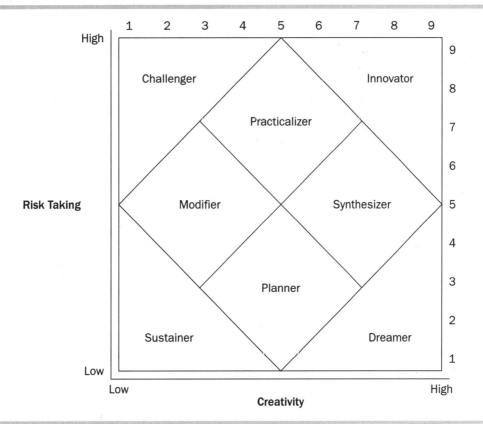

The Orientations

Now let's talk about each of the eight orientations shown on the Creatrix grid in detail. We'll look at their value to your organization, their limitations, and, most importantly, how you can work with them to begin building your organization's and/or team's innovative capacity.

The Creatrix, as shown in Figure 2.2, is divided into eight zones, each of which represents an innovation orientation based on one's creativity and risk-taking results.

The vertical scale of the Creatrix designates whether the respondent is a low, moderate, or high *risk taker*; the horizontal scale designates overall *creative abilities*.

Take a moment to study the illustration. Note that scoring very high on *both* the creativity and risk-taking scales puts the respondent into the Innovator category.

This means that a combination of risk-taking and creative behaviors enables the person to have the greatest capacity for innovation. It does *not* necessarily mean that he or she will provide the greatest value to an organization; nor does it mean that people with lower scores on each of the scales have less to offer the organization. Each orientation has its own strengths and limitations.

People with every one of these orientations contribute something valuable to an organization or team. The beauty of a highly functioning organization is that it has individuals whose orientations are represented by several or even all of the orientations. Organizations require balance, and if an entire team were composed of nothing but Innovators or Sustainers, it would be highly dysfunctional.

Let us explain in more detail. For example, Innovators have the unique ability to come up with a virtually unlimited number of new ideas. However, one of the limitations of the Innovator is that he or she does not realize what it takes to follow through on each of these great ideas. On the opposite end of the scale is the Sustainer, someone who is great at doing voluminous amounts of routine work. Coupled together, the Innovator and Sustainer make a remarkably powerful combination.

By learning about each of the eight orientations in detail, you'll begin to learn how to take advantage of each orientation's strengths. You'll discover how to build a powerfully innovative organization, how to shape the right team for the right job, and how to minimize its inherent limitations. Let's look at each of the orientations in detail.

The Challenger

Challengers are high risk takers and often straightforward and outspoken in their style. They are low in creativity but understand the need for risk.

Value to Organizations

Challengers are consistent risk takers. They serve the organization in any area in which ineffective, inefficient, or improper methods or processes are being used. Although they don't often create the new ideas, they become discontent when change is slow. They provide an important contribution by exposing sacred cows. For example, management may create a climate in which certain programs are not discussed or in which people or programs that have long overstayed their welcome are tolerated. The Challenger will openly ask, "What's going on here?" In a group situation, the Challenger is the person who presents an excellent analysis of why something will not work. The Challenger's energy lies in wait for the really creative idea by a Dreamer who may not be willing to take a risk.

Avoiding the Challenger is often a preferred strategy for those in the organization without well-formulated ideas. But while Challengers cloak themselves in the role of the cynic, deep down lies a person who truly wants success for the teams he or she plays on. The value of the self-ordained Challenger is in his or her ability to quickly expose the erroneous efforts of others. And while this is off-putting to many, the organization is indeed better off for these critical ways.

Hindrances to Organizations

Because Challengers believe in telling it like it is, they may destroy where destruction is not needed. For example, they may advocate breeching a long-term relationship and contract to make way for the new, not realizing the many by-products of tenured clients and vendors. Any program that needs time to prove itself may not receive the chance if Challengers are allowed to set the tone. Sometimes they appear to want change for its own sake. The value and hindrances of Challengers are presented in Table 2.1.

Table 2.1. Challenger Profile

Primary Motivations	Value to Organization	Limitations
Self-motivated and self-directed	When tolerant, provides excellent critiques	Often can be viewed as critical
Waiting for the really creative idea	Exposes sacred cows	May miss the really creative ideas

An Example of a Challenger

Charlie was the next in line to become CEO for LLS, Inc. The only thing holding the board back from voting for him was that he was a Challenger. The board made statements like these:

- His directness can be too harsh;
- He lacks respect for others' feeling and emotions—he runs right over people; and
- He sometimes asks the wrong questions.

After learning about his Creatrix orientation and understanding that his nature to challenge was well-intended, they voted for Charlie to become the next CEO. The board agreed that:

- You always know where Charlie stands (you may not like it but at least you always know);

- He speaks his mind, but also allows you to speak your mind; and

- He is a good negotiator. He's willing to take risks in order to get the job done.

The Sustainer

Sustainers offer stability. They provide much-needed practical reality in times of change. They maintain the tried-and-true because the past generally holds the best lessons.

Value to Organizations

Sustainers are often the backbone of an organization and provide the control and predictive functions that are necessary for good management. They usually support control methods, standardization, time studies, industrial engineering methods, quality control, and simplicity of product lines. Because most situations demand some repetition, Sustainers are not offended by repetitive tasks that people with other orientations might find boring. Despite the fact that many organizations could not exist without them, Sustainers often do not receive the appreciation they deserve.

The Sustainer is the backbone of the organization and, like the backbone in our bodies, the Sustainer is rarely appreciated until a dull ache indicating something's askew harkens the organization's attention. Capable of producing voluminous amounts of repetitious work, Sustainers provide the necessary nourishment to keep the organization running. Without the continuity and stability provided by the Sustainers, the organization would be continually shifting to the whims of the Innovator or Synthesizer, who often forget the value of "sustaining."

Coupling Sustainers with persons from virtually any of the other seven orientations makes a powerful combination, yielding the dynamic results of applied innovation.

Hindrances to Organizations

Sustainers sometimes become stuck in ruts. When change occurs, they may continue to perform tasks that no longer need to be done. They often resist new systems and techniques. They attempt to use old methods for the new tasks. They will block change, not out of malice, but because they are unable to see the value of changing. Their qualities are summarized in Table 2.2.

Table 2.2. Sustainer Profile

Primary Motivations	Value to Organization	Hindrances to Organization
Control	Ability to do voluminous amounts of routine work	Continue to perform tasks that are no longer required
Standardization	Often knows exactly what's required to get the job done	Unable to see alternatives/options

An Example of a Sustainer

Samantha had been the assistant for the partners for over twelve years. She never missed a day of work and was always on time. Her typing was impeccable and her attention to detail was second to none. But several new initiatives were being introduced into the company and R.J., one of the partners, wanted Samantha to take on some new responsibilities. This required her to change her work schedule and work three days in one office and two days in another. In addition, she'd have to supervise a couple of new people and do different types of tasks—things she hadn't done before. R.J. thought that she'd be excited at the chance to take on new responsibilities. He was taken aback when she:

- Tried to talk him out of the new initiatives, saying that they weren't necessary and that everything was working fine;
- Complained about working in different offices;
- Said she didn't want more responsibility; and
- Asked why it couldn't be like the old days.

Samantha just didn't seem to want to adjust, so R.J. had to find someone else to take the position and Samantha continued to work for the other partner. To her credit she continued showing up on time, producing a quality product, and keeping the wheels of the old organization moving while the new initiatives were getting off the ground.

The Innovator

Innovators are very high on both risk taking and creativity. Most major nonincremental successes in American industry are the result of Innovators. Henry Ford is perhaps the most commonly used example of a man with an idea. But men like Bill

Gates and Ted Turner appear at the top of the contemporary list of Innovators. They are not afraid to take risks. In fact, from most people's point of view, Innovators will risk more than they can afford to lose. They always have a new idea. To others, the Innovator seems just like the Challenger: outspoken, hard to influence, and of a single mind. Unlike the Challenger, however, the Innovator always has a better mousetrap.

Value to Organizations

Innovators can sense breakthrough products, which must be accepted from time to time if an organization is to remain viable. Initially, their breakthroughs may be unpopular because they involve new technology and various kinds of changes. Innovators are aware of this fact and will fight fiercely for the breakthrough's acceptance. Although usually admired and often feared, Innovators are viewed as radicals and are rarely at the head of the most-liked list. Innovators continue to believe in their ideas when no one else does. When their ideas are not accepted in an organization, Innovators frequently look for capital to start their own companies.

The Innovator's unique blend of high levels of both creativity and risk taking frequently stirs up mixed emotions from the rest of us. Seemingly always on the cutting edge of new ideas and showing little fear, the Innovator is both inspiring to others and loathed for numerous brash attempts at making improvements in the organization. Yet it is the Innovator who has the courage to venture into unchartered waters and discover new lands, never fearing having lost sight of the shore. The value the Innovator brings to the company is magnified greatly when tempered with members from other orientations whose aversion to unlimited creativity and risk taking counterbalance the efforts of the Innovator, thereby affording the organization the opportunity to take advantage of grounding the latest and greatest for implementation.

Hindrances to Organizations

Innovators may become so fixed on an idea that they are not willing to wait until the time is right. Innovators feel so strongly about certain potential breakthroughs that they cannot see the implementation problems. When what they want is not forthcoming, they may develop a paranoia that the organization is against them or that others are plotting their demise. The benefits and hindrances are summarized in Table 2.3.

Table 2.3. Innovator Profile

Primary Motivations	Value to Organization	Hindrances to Organization
Breakthrough creations	Always has a better mousetrap	Hard to influence (of a single mind)
Self-motivated	Will keep an organization always questioning its focus—on its toes	May risk more than they or the company can afford to lose

An Example of an Innovator

Scott was head of a major new initiative that the company had launched. People were both excited and afraid to have Scott at the helm. In the hallways people made such comments as the following:

- His ideas are absolutely wonderful, but he expects everyone to agree to adopt them right away.

- He doesn't know when to give it a rest. He just keeps spitting the ideas out without letting the first one develop. He moves on to the next one and wonders why we haven't finished it yet. We've got to have time to implement too!

- He's constantly breaking all the rules and making up new ones "to adapt to our rapidly changing competitive marketplace."

As time passed, his colleagues couldn't have been more pleased with Scott because his contributions added to the success of the company. By the time the competition countered with their new product idea, Scott already had his in prototype. He surrounded himself with people who were just as innovative as he was, and it added to the number of new ideas, threefold. While he didn't always follow all of the rules, some of the rules made it impossible to get things done, and his willingness to "color outside of the lines" made both him and the new initiative successful.

The Dreamer

Dreamers are high on creativity and low on risk taking. They are the comfortable creative types. Dreamers always have lots of ideas.

Value to Organizations

The most underutilized people within an organization are the Dreamers. Their heads are full of unusual ideas but, because of their lack of aggressiveness, their ideas may look like crackpot schemes to the more conventional. Dreamers fit well in jobs that require planning, demand little risk taking, and provide time to think. Dreamers are most beneficial to an organization when their supervisors are Practicalizers. Since the talents of Dreamers can be described as unmined gold, some other force is needed to implement their original ideas. At home, the Dreamers may be inventors or just someone who tinkers all of the time.

Vital in their ability to create and bring beauty to life, the Dreamers often are the artists of this world. Their unique ability to paint a landscape, write a song, or spin a tall tale creates the necessary diversions from the stresses of reality. In an organization, it's the Dreamer who often has innovative answers, yet they are rarely volunteered because the Dreamer sees the value of the idea as its own reward. One would be wise to solicit the ideas of the Dreamer frequently, for it is here that innovation lies in wait. Leaders of organizations are further cautioned to refrain from needlessly prodding the seemingly idle Dreamer to come to task because it is quite likely that solutions to the organization's most pressing problems reside here.

Hindrances to Organizations

The major weakness is obvious: Dreamers underachieve. They always have a better idea, but rarely suggest it unless asked for it. Dreamers are discontent in organizations that they know could grow faster by using their ideas, but they are afraid to risk it and try to convince the company that their approaches are better. Being so reticent, they may set regressive patterns that make the risk-taking orientations of the organization's Challengers, Practicalizers, and Innovators seem even more risky. Their pluses and minuses are summarized in Table 2.4.

Table 2.4. Dreamer Profile

Primary Motivations	Value to Organization	Hindrances to Organization
Creating and tinkering	Talents are unmined gold	The idea in and of itself is enough reward to define success
Likes to have time to think	Source of virtually unlimited ideas	Afraid to open up and suggest their ideas

An Example of a Dreamer

"What does Dick think about your situation, Bill?"

"I don't know, I haven't mentioned it to him yet."

"You know it might not be a bad idea to talk to him."

"I guess I never really considered Dick's opinion—he's so quiet."

"Dick may be quiet because:

- He doesn't really care whether anyone knows about his ideas;

- He just likes to tinker and come up with new things and his garage is full of neat stuff that he's made; or

- He always has a better mousetrap, but you have to ask him about it because he's not inclined to volunteer the information."

"Consider it done. After all, I really need some help on this project. I'm sure Dick will be able to come up with numerous ideas after he's had a chance to reflect on our situation and help some of the other business units that are stuck with doing the same old things."

The Modifier

Modifiers are moderately creative and moderate on risk taking. They take what is and add to it. Modifiers can virtually take anything and make it better.

Value to Organizations

Modifiers can usually be counted on for the constant little improvements so necessary for lowering the costs of production, marketing, and management. They may suggest turning a form from portrait to landscape for easier use, changing the shape of a mold, or using different types of materials. They may move two machines closer together so that one person can operate both at the same time or add paragraphs to a manuscript. Because their proposed alterations are rarely threatening to others, they are usually liked. Modifiers are usually valued by their organizations. They provide safe, incremental improvements.

The Modifier is the contributor who makes the suggestions for slight incremental improvements that no one else sees. Organizations are virtually always better with Modifiers on board. They have suggestions to improve on an idea, but operate within limits in which they're willing to work. The Modifier works well alongside those with other higher risk-taking and creative orientations who seem to be constantly in search of that "innovative idea," who then only need to look to the Modifier for that little twist that makes all the difference.

Hindrances to Organizations

Modifiers won't come up with the "brilliant solutions," but they will come up with the incremental solutions. Modifiers will take moderate risks and implement them. However, if management wants something "the old way," Modifiers are willing to return to doing it that way. Like Sustainers, they won't fight very hard for their own suggestions. This has drawbacks for the organization. The modification they are proposing may have major cost efficiencies or technological advantages, but Modifiers' lower propensity for risk taking in the face of challenge or adversity will cause them to back off in many situations in which they are really challenged. See the summary in Table 2.5.

Table 2.5. Modifier Profile

Primary Motivations	Value to Organization	Hindrances to Organization
Minor improvements	Virtually constant incremental improvements	Backs off when challenged—doesn't want to take the risk
Better operations	Tweaks systems in such a way as to make a difference	May want to modify when a major breakthrough is required

An Example of a Modifier

Having just been made division vice president, Marilyn was ready to take on a new challenge. But she didn't want to shake things up too much. She wanted to lead her division to new heights, but she wanted to be cautious in her approach. She took the following actions:

- Adjusted the division's financial goals to represent improvements, albeit incremental and achievable;

- Consolidated departments to eliminate duplication of effort; and

- Introduced one new initiative to the organization's strategic plan.

Given the economic conditions and competitive climate, Marilyn's plan worked because:

- She knew the capability of her team and stretched them within reason;
- She added value to a system that needed some changes made, but not too many; and
- She improved both the top and bottom line of her division, thereby helping the organization meet its superordinate goals.

The Practicalizer

Practicalizers are high on risk taking and moderately creative. Although they are no more creative than the Planner, they make ideas work because they will take more risks.

Value to Organizations

Practicalizers are action-oriented. They accomplish what they set out to do. Often they are the only ones who can get a change accepted. They are confident of their ability to produce. President Lyndon B. Johnson said, "Politics is the arena of the possible," and Practicalizers are the organization's politicians. They are rarely confused between the right thing to do creatively and what can be implemented. Practicalizers are confident that they will be able to convince top management of the need to make major changes. Practicalizers are usually perceived as effective managers. They like taking ideas and driving them through the bureaucratic walls of the organization. Because they are moderately creative, they recognize the gifts of the Innovator (who tends to be socially less acceptable) and of the Synthesizer, Dreamer, and Planner (who are preoccupied with the product/idea rather than its implementation).

Practicalizers are the ones who recognize a creative idea and can make it happen. However, the idea must have practical merit, be actionable, and have clear deliverables. Thus, their risk taking is grounded in reality and not in possibility. The Practicalizer knows how to make what may seem like fluff and nonsense to some become pragmatic and successful.

Hindrances to Organizations

Perhaps the major weakness of Practicalizers is that they run right over ideas of the super-creative person in a crunch because the ideas may not be practical. Consequently, Practicalizers sometimes miss the big payoff. These qualities are summarized in Table 2.6.

Table 2.6. Practicalizer Profile

Primary Motivations	Value to Organization	Hindrances to Organization
Confident in ability to produce	Knows how to drive ideas through bureaucratic walls of the organization	May squelch initially improbable ideas
Results-oriented	Gets it done—takes action	May miss the big payoff

An Example of a Practicalizer

Peter had been firm with everyone that the paper business was drying up. He believed that they had to reposition the company into new businesses that could survive the ups and downs. Paper was just too volatile. He rolled out a new strategic plan. His leadership team reacted negatively to the ideas he was proposing. They thought:

- Peter's ideas might fly, but he is taking too high a risk;
- He needs to move more slowly, as the rest of the organization isn't able to come along as fast as he is moving; and
- He is too confident that it will work.

Two years later it was clear that if Peter hadn't seen the practical application of the move:

- The company would have been in deep trouble, as their core business line had very soft sales, and
- A few people who had actually backed Peter up on his original strategic decision said that he could have gone further if "he had only listened to our ideas too!"

The Synthesizer

Synthesizers are quite creative and moderate to high in taking risks. They are idea people. They have a unique ability to blend conceptually the ideas of others.

Value to Organizations

Synthesizers take unlikely combinations of people, programs, or products and devise a new entity. Their talents are in taking other people's ideas, adding their own, and then making those ideas fit into any situation, regardless of the circumstances. Their ideas may never be as practical or as easily implemented as those of the Practicalizer, but they will develop high-quality ideas that are just short of a breakthrough. They see combinations of functions, processes, and people that others do not see. New organization charts or production flows challenge their ingenuity. Synthesizers continually combine the needs of the customer with the organization's talents and resources. They are socialized Innovators. If there is no Innovator, then the Synthesizer's new ideas, always appealing and usually marketable, will prevail.

Synthesizers are all over—taking information in here and there and reapplying it to completely unique situations that others wouldn't have thought of. Synthesizers are always scanning the environment for opportunities and, if it means breaking the rules, they're ready to do it. Synthesizers will look at all the other orientations and say, "What do you have that I can use?" Watch what happens when you throw them a loose end!

Hindrances to Organization

The major blind spot of Synthesizers is an inability to risk all for a breakthrough. They believe in incremental breakthroughs. They believe that the ideas will carry their own weight to produce change. This position makes them appear to be Dreamers or Planners to those who do not understand how far Synthesizers will go to sell their ideas. Their qualities are summarized in Table 2.7.

Table 2.7. Synthesizer Profile

Primary Motivations	Value to Organization	Hindrances to Organization
Quality	Combines needs of customers with organization's talents and resources	Can be confusing and misunderstood
Self-directed	Produces unimaginable synergies	May fall short of truly innovative breakthroughs

An Example of a Synthesizer

Susan walked into the room. "I've got a great idea," she said. "If we were to tap into the work that is being done by XYZ, Inc., and Omega-First Industries and then add our own spin to it, we'd have an ad campaign that would knock their socks off." People around the table:

- Looked at her like she was crazy and wondered how the work being done by XYZ, Inc., and Omega-First related at all to their work and

- Wanted to believe that it was possible, as they knew that she was highly creative, but it just seemed too unbelievable.

Indeed, people had seen the work that had come from Susan over the years, so they'd learned to trust the fact that:

- She saw linkages that no one else did;

- Her ideas, even when they seemed off the wall, had opened up lots of possibilities in the past; and

- When they didn't try to understand Susan, they'd often see her ideas show up somewhere else—usually in the competition's backyard.

The Planner

Planners score as moderate on the creativity scale and low on risk taking. They want creative ideas to be operable, but not with undue risk.

Value to Organizations

Planners think of ways in which creative ideas might be utilized. Usually they are respected for their contributions because they develop alternatives for an organization. They have the ability to write corporate roadmaps and to design management and operational systems. They make good staff people and provide appropriate caution. They often fit well in a planning department, an architectural firm, a consulting firm, or a teaching position.

Planners create frameworks that others wish they could create but usually don't. While others may be hasty, the Planner is deliberate, asking people to demonstrate and show the evidence of why or why not. They operate wisely and cautiously and offer the upsides and downsides of an opportunity, advising some of the other orientations not to "jump too quickly" and not to take the risk before planning the alternatives. If an answer that spells out what and why something will work or not work is desired, people need only to call on the Planner to assist them. People use their expertise for success.

Hindrances to Organizations

Planners are not action-oriented and will generally avoid taking risks. Even though they are more creative than Modifiers, they will rarely take the risks that Modifiers take, even though they are sold on an idea. Planners tend to be other-directed. Like Practicalizers, Planners want creative ideas to be operable, but they may not have the necessary risk-taking capacity to push them through. The result is that Planners can make the plans, but cannot force them through the channels. These characteristics are summarized in Table 2.8.

Table 2.8. Planner Profile

Primary Motivations	Value to Organization	Hindrances to Organization
Wants creative ideas to be operable	Respected for their contributions	Rarely action-oriented
Order and structure	Have the ability to write corporate roadmaps and to design management and operational systems	Usually avoid risks; stick to the plan, even to their own detriment

An Example of a Planner

John called Paula into the discussion: "The ideas are flowing like crazy, but we need your help, Paula. You always bring structure and order to the chaos. You don't always have to add your two-cents worth; you can just take what everyone else is coming up with and add clarity to what needs to happen. You add rationality to the table by helping us think about how the new ideas fit, or conversely, don't fit within our current plan."

Paula liked her role in the organization, but sometimes worried that:

- She might be too much of a stickler for "staying within plan";
- She didn't add the same value as some of the more creative people in the organization; and
- She might appear too structured to some, almost rigid.

Table 2.9 highlights the key attributes of each of the eight orientations. You can see the differences at a glance and begin to understand a fuller range of creativity and risk-taking perspectives.

Table 2.9. Highlights of the Eight Orientations

Challengers

Have the attitude of "do it"; if we do nothing we will lose out

Take others' ideas and drive them home

Get excited about new ideas but seldom create their own

Can take on too many ideas and not see them to fruition

Sustainers

Like stability and do not seek change

Do voluminous amounts of routine work

Hold an organization accountable and true to its mission

Don't like to take chances or offer many ideas

Keep the organization "humming"

Modifiers

Believe incremental changes are okay

Will frequently improve things by tweaking them

Like to test the waters before doing anything

Don't take risks unless they can see the real benefits over leaving things the same

Synthesizers

Will drive an idea home, but not at all costs; are more cautious than Innovators

Create by putting things together—things that may even be unlikely bedfellows

See possibilities in everything

Innovators

Have a new idea every minute

Think more highly of their own ideas than others'

Always think they can figure out how they can make it happen

Keep an organization off balance—not usually a good thing

Can hit the "grand slam"

Dreamers

Can be the creative juices for an organization as long as they hook up with a type that can drive their ideas

Let most of their ideas die because they cannot figure out how to make them happen

Are creative; constantly are coming up with new ways to do things

Practicalizers

Like changes, but not too many at once

Are willing to try something new

Will come up with creative ideas, but do not consider this their forte

Help the organization continue to grow by pushing it along

Planners

Believe that an idea has merit if it fits within "the plan"

Come up with creative ideas within known parameters

Need information and data before taking a risk

Changing Orientations

Can one change orientation? Can a Planner become a Synthesizer, or can a Modifier become a Planner or Practicalizer? The answer is yes. Although it is probably difficult, if not impossible, to move from being a Sustainer to an Innovator, orientations can be changed. So why would one want to change? Because becoming more creative and taking more risks helps a person to develop himself or herself and further contributes to the innovative capacity of an organization.

But people may like themselves just the way they are and may be happy with the description of your creativity and risk-taking orientation. Each orientation contributes something and people may already be making the kinds of contributions that they and their organization value.

To reshape an organization for innovative success, one must first understand the eight orientations and what each brings to the table. One must find out the current composition of the organization or team and then restructure to achieve a balance in their makeup. We will talk about this in detail in Chapter 6.

Another way to change the shape of the organization is to move each person on a team in an incrementally northeast direction (except the Innovator, who actually may want to move in a southwestern direction). The dynamics of having each person move just slightly higher on each of the scales has an exponential effect on the organization's innovative capacity, even if the improvement is only slight in individual cases. But how can individuals move in a northeasterly direction? The drivers of creativity and risk taking, discussed in the next chapter, are the keys to building innovative capacity throughout the organization.

Ideas for the Consultant

If working with teams or setting the stage for working with an entire organization:

- Discuss the value of being able to measure innovation.

- Ask people to identify and share stories about their orientations. Do they fit? Why or why not?

- Discuss the value of each orientation. Explain the value and hindrances of each orientation to the organization. Emphasize the contributions that are made by each orientation.

- Provide examples of when and why you need different orientations (the northeast corner orientations foster innovation, the southwest corner orientations are good implementers). Or ask who they'd put on a team given a specific task—developing a new product or service.

- Ask people to identify others outside their current team/organization who exemplify the different orientations. This helps to create a shared understanding of each of the orientations.

- Discuss teams or organizations that exemplify one of the orientations. Give an example of a Challenger team (venture capital groups) or a Planner organization (universities).

3

The Drivers of Creativity and Risk Taking

"No one can give another person challenge, adventure, motivation, a competitive spirit, a sense of personal fulfillment, drive, purpose, and ingenuity. Each individual either demands a working environment that permits those motivations to be realized or takes the risk to go elsewhere."

Richard E. Byrd, A Guide to Personal Risk Taking

IT IS NOT ENOUGH to want to become more creative and to take more risks. To do so means challenging yourself, your team, the organization. Moving out of our comfort zone is something that we're not always excited about doing. Yet it is when we move out of our comfort zones that we find ourselves gaining insights into our own character, and at that point we are able to remold and reshape ourselves to the way we want. This is also the case with organizations and teams. But it means changing the culture of the organization or team.

Every organization or team has a culture. This culture is reflected in what the organization or team values and how it goes about doing its business, as well as its propensity for risk taking and creativity. Think about the organization or team you work for or in. How does it view risk taking? Does your culture punish or reward people for taking risks? What is your personal willingness to take risks in your current organization? As you answer these questions, you might begin to realize that part of your individual behavior is a function of the environment or culture. For example, you might be willing to take greater risks, but because the person you report to doles out punitive measures for anyone who fails at even the slightest task, you begin to curb your willingness. Or consider when someone offers an unconventional idea at a brainstorming session and some eyes roll and heavy sighs are heard. What is the likelihood that the same person might think twice about offering another idea before the group?

Thus, the creativity and risk taking evidenced collectively in an organization's or team's culture is consistent with the characteristics of one of the orientations: Challenger, Innovator, Dreamer, Sustainer, Planner, Modifier, Practicalizer, or Innovator. This composite profile of the organization or team becomes the group's orientation—or group norm. So we can describe one group as a Challenger group and another as a Planner group, and they take on the attributes of these orientations.

If you think changing the creativity and risk-taking profiles of individuals is difficult, consider that change in an organization and team is often far more difficult because you're trying to increase the innovative capacity of more than one person. Remember, however, what we said in Chapter 1: Individuals are motivated both to create and to take risks. Knowledge of this intrinsic drive is what makes change possible in organizations. That's why it's important to work the process at all levels. That is, work needs to be done at the individual, team, *and* organization level in order to realize the greatest benefit. Since many of us do not have the ability to influence the organization as a whole, we need to concentrate our efforts on what we do have influence over: our immediate work teams and ourselves. Efforts made in these areas can yield powerful results that may ultimately reverberate throughout the entire organization.

The Drivers

Changing our individual, team, or organizational innovation orientation begins with knowing what drives risk-taking and creative behavior. There are seven drivers of creativity and risk taking: four that drive creativity and three that drive risk taking. The seven drivers are depicted in Table 3.1.

Table 3.1. The Seven Drivers of Creativity and Risk Taking

Creativity Drivers	Risk-Taking Drivers
Ambiguity	Authenticity
Independence	Resiliency
Inner-Directedness	Self-Acceptance
Uniqueness	

If you want to build greater innovative capacity, you can use these drivers of creativity and risk taking. In the remainder of this chapter, we show you how.

Before we take a closer look at each of these drivers, let's begin by contrasting each of the drivers with its polar opposite. In Table 3.2 below, the descriptors in the right-hand column are the drivers for greater innovation. The descriptors in the left-hand column are the inhibitors of innovation.

Table 3.2. Inhibitors and Corresponding Drivers of Innovation

Inhibitors	Drivers
Demanding of Predictability	Accepting of Ambiguity
Dependent	Independent
Other-Directed	Inner-Directed
Conforming	Unique
Political	Authentic
Rigid	Resilient
Victimized	Self-Accepting

Creativity Driver = Ambiguity and Its Opposite, Predictability

Being able to operate in an ambiguous situation means you must be able to deal with uncertainty and vagueness. Individuals, teams, or organizations that function effectively in ambiguous circumstances don't require highly structured situations, goals, or objectives to accomplish or create things, ideas, services, or products. The opposite of ambiguity is *predictability.* People who demand predictability require a great deal of structure, clarity, and definition, regardless of the problem being addressed. By definition they are unable to deal with ambiguous situations.

Effectively dealing with ambiguous situations is perhaps the one area where corporate America has the most trouble. Many individuals and organizations go to great lengths to control variables, chart alternative courses of action, and eliminate the impact of uncertainty. Growth in this one area alone yields tremendous results in terms of being able to come up with innovative solutions.

Creativity Driver = Independence and Its Opposite, Dependence

Independence means not subject to the control, influence, or determination of another or others. The opposite of being independent is being *dependent* on others. Dependent people always need direction from someone else. They do not take action without prior approval. People who are independent will not subordinate themselves to others. They don't like to be managed by others. They are self-empowered. It's clear that individuals or teams that operate with independence don't like working for anyone else; they also don't have to be given direction. This can be a manager's dream or a nightmare. Independent individuals or teams can get into trouble because they don't like to ask for help and they consider their way to be the best way.

Creativity Driver = Inner-Directedness and Its Opposite, Other-Directedness

Inner-directed people, teams, or organizations feel a great sense of purpose. They often have a clear vision of the future. People who are inner-directed believe that they are responsible for determining their own destiny. Its opposite is being other-directed. People who are *other-directed* are always concerned about what everyone else thinks or is doing. Other-directed people don't take the lead without input from others. Inner-directedness is the ability to determine one's own expectations and norms. Inner-directed people, teams, and organizations march to the beat of their own drummers. They are guided by their own set of values rather than someone else's norms. They value this quality and sometimes believe that no one "really" understands them. Often, inner-directed people have difficulty in large organizations. Reconciling personal agendas to corporate directives can sometimes be an impossible task.

Creativity Driver = Uniqueness and Its Opposite, Conformity

Uniqueness is appreciating and valuing differences, both in oneself and in others. People, teams, and organizations that value uniqueness look for creativity in themselves and in others. They actually foster it because it is such an important driver for them. They first and foremost see and look for the differences in others and, in fact, will look for differences over similarities. They don't necessarily look for differences to accentuate them; they simply see them and know how to appreciate and take advantage of them. They value inventors over virtually anyone else. The opposite of uniqueness is *conformity*. People who are conforming act in a way that conforms to the current styles, norms, or expectations.

Risk-Taking Driver = Authentic and Its Opposite, Political

Authentic means being what you purport to be. Authentic people, teams, and organizations believe that living by their core beliefs is the most important and highest value; they mean what they say and say what they mean. Their actions are congruent with their espoused values. Its opposite is being *political.* Political people are unable to communicate with others directly. They are always navigating or positioning for self-advantage. Authenticity is about being genuine. Sometimes people refer to authentic people as "walking their talk" and "telling it like it is." You may not always like what the authentic person says, but you always know where he or she stands on an issue. The one thing you know about authentic people is that they are true to themselves.

Risk-Taking Driver = Resiliency and Its Opposite, Rigidity

Resiliency is the ability to rebound, successfully adapt, and learn, even in the face of adversity and stress. Resilient people have the ability to pick themselves up after being knocked down. They have the attitude that something good always comes out of a bad experience. From any experience, they're able to create options—they know that there's always a way out and they will find it. Its opposite is *rigidity.* Rigidity is represented by inflexibility, especially in response to change, rejection, or setbacks. Resilient people persevere in the face of adversity. They get the job done, sometimes by the force of their own will.

Risk-Taking Driver = Self-Acceptance and Its Opposite, Victimization

Self-accepting means to be approving of or satisfied with one's own behaviors or actions. Self-accepting people like themselves and their situations. They exhibit a self-confidence that is often perceived as a challenge to some and a wonder to others. Self-accepting people are unlikely to say they're sorry about much, because they usually don't have many regrets. Its opposite is *victimization.* Victimized people complain and blame others. Self-accepting people don't try to be perfect because they are clearly aware that it's not even possible. They like themselves, in spite of themselves sometimes.

Innovative Capacity Continuum

Ask yourself this general question: "What impact would it have within my organization or team if I made it my goal to truly embody the nature of one of these drivers?" for example, becoming more independent or more authentic. Imagine then, what would happen if everybody within the organization or the team were to make the same commitment. The innovative capacity of the organization would accelerate.

Let's take a moment to view the Innovative Capacity Continuum. Exhibit 3.1 is an example of an individual and his organization's profile on the drivers. This continuum helps individuals contrast their propensity for creativity and risk taking with the organization or team as a whole. It serves as a foundation from which valuable dialogue can occur with respect to changing the organization's paradigms toward greater innovation through creativity and risk taking. Notice the different levels of creativity and risk taking when contrasting the individual with the organization. In this case, the individual assessed himself as more innovative on most scales than the organization. In some cases, individuals (especially those in positions of authority and power) can inhibit the organization, while at other times the organization can inhibit creative individuals who are willing to take greater risks.

Exhibit 3.1. Sample Innovative Capacity Continuum Results

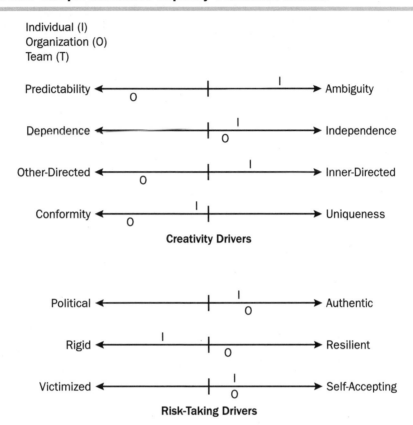

Individual (I)
Organization (O)
Team (T)

Predictability ◄————————————► Ambiguity
Dependence ◄————————————► Independence
Other-Directed ◄————————————► Inner-Directed
Conformity ◄————————————► Uniqueness

Creativity Drivers

Political ◄————————————► Authentic
Rigid ◄————————————► Resilient
Victimized ◄————————————► Self-Accepting

Risk-Taking Drivers

Now we invite you to plot where you see yourself and your organization or team along the continuum shown in Exhibit 3.2. Consider the midpoint on each continuum as neutral. Use an I for yourself and a T or O, depending on whether you are plotting a team you're working in or your organization as a whole.

Exhibit 3.2. Your Innovative Capacity Continuum Results

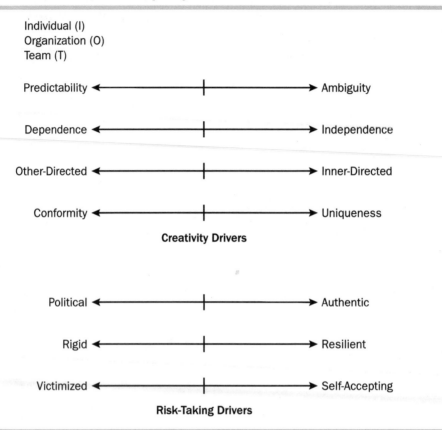

Individual (I)
Organization (O)
Team (T)

Predictability ◄——————————┼——————————► Ambiguity

Dependence ◄——————————┼——————————► Independence

Other-Directed ◄——————————┼——————————► Inner-Directed

Conformity ◄——————————┼——————————► Uniqueness

Creativity Drivers

Political ◄——————————┼——————————► Authentic

Rigid ◄——————————┼——————————► Resilient

Victimized ◄——————————┼——————————► Self-Accepting

Risk-Taking Drivers

Developing a greater awareness of these drivers and how the organization, team, or individual can be plotted on the Innovative Capacity Continuum is essential for building innovation. For example, if I have difficulty dealing with ambiguity, I'll find myself seeking to bring greater levels of clarity in virtually all situations in order for me to be comfortable; this need for predictability (the opposite of ambiguity) limits my potential range of creative responses.

It is important, therefore, to plot both your organization and yourself on the continuum in order to determine which driver would be the most valuable to focus on. Take the "Driver Quick-Check" in Exhibit 3.3 to help you determine which creativity or risk-taking driver(s) you may need to focus on for building innovative capacity.

Exhibit 3.3. Driver Quick-Check

Creativity Drivers	Frequently	Sometimes	Occasionally	Seldom
Ambiguity *I can make decisions without all the facts.*				
Independence *I don't need others to tell me what to do.*				
Inner-Directed *I listen to and trust my inner self.*				
Uniqueness *I value the unique contributions of myself and others.*				

Risk-Taking Drivers

Authenticity *I tell it like it is.*				
Resiliency *I bounce back from almost anything.*				
Self-Acceptance *I tell myself: I'm OK with who I am.*				

Check marks in the occasionally or seldom columns indicate drivers that you may want to focus on. We'd suggest selecting just one at a time. Working on one driver can be powerful; three or more can frustrate and overwhelm you or a team. Increasing innovative capacity is a function of activating these drivers. Let's look at a few stories and see what these drivers are all about in an organization.

Creativity Driver Stories

Ambiguity at Work

"Keeping your mind open in the face of uncertainty is the single most powerful secret of unleashing your creative potential."

Leonardo da Vinci quoted in Michael J. Gelb,
How to Think Like Leonardo da Vinci

▶ A STORY OF AMBIGUITY

Word had just been received at headquarters that the competition was going to release their new product next quarter. Being first to market in the electronics industry is half the battle. The timing couldn't have been worse. Just the other day, the R&D department reported difficulty in resolving the production run problems in their Far East facilities. It looked like it was going to be six months before they could retool; this meant the competition was going to beat them to market this time. Missing the scheduled product launch date would likely mean a shakeup for the key personnel who were responsible. An alternative would be to start production and omit the new feature; this would mean getting to market first, but with an inferior product—clearly an undesirable alternative. The final choice would be to start production using a new technology that had yet to be beta tested in volume.

Anthony, the CEO, didn't quite know what to do. He knew the competition had missed launch dates before. He also knew he could shave some time off the retooling schedule, but didn't think he could cut it in half! Everyone knew starting production without beta testing was simply asking for trouble.

Like the old adage says, sometimes it is indeed lonely at the top. Anthony narrowly missed his first year's earnings estimate and that took a heavy toll on the stock price. Another untimely error in judgment might very well point to the end of an otherwise meteoric career rise.

Anthony followed his hunches; what else could he do? He banked on the fact that he knew he could shave some time off the scheduled six-month retooling. He also played a bet that the competition would likely miss their rollout date, even if only by a few weeks. The gamble paid off. He shaved a month off the retooling efforts, and the competition was indeed late in their product release. Anthony couldn't foresee the results, but nonetheless had to pick what he thought was the best course of action. And although Anthony's company wasn't first to market, an aggressive ad campaign hyping the new product release only ten days behind the competition had virtually the same overall effect as a simultaneous product launch date.

The lessons here are simple. Sometimes we have to act without having all of the information. The question is how we respond in such situations? Are we frozen in "paralysis of analysis"? Or do we rise to the occasion, chart a course, and roll with the punches? Learning how to deal with ambiguity is an important element in fostering creativity. ◄

Some well-known personalities who seem to exhibit acceptance of ambiguity include people like Bill Clinton, Jack Welch, and Ehud Barak. When speaking with people who tolerate high levels of ambiguity, you're likely to hear phrases like: "Hindsight is always 20/20" or "Let's just do the best we can with the information we have."

Independence at Work

"You must do the thing you think you cannot do."

Eleanor Roosevelt

► A STORY OF INDEPENDENCE

Fresh out of graduate school and after a brief two-year stint as a consultant, Ingrid found herself at the crossroads of life (again!). She wasn't happy at her job. Oh sure, the pay was OK, but it wasn't what she knew she could make if she had a chance to strike out on her own. Without a book of clients and with only enough savings to last a minor economic drought, Ingrid faced a challenging decision. Should she hang out her own shingle—go out on her own? Or should she hold tight to her reasonably good, albeit largely unsatisfying, consulting gig?

Ingrid didn't usually consult with a personal board of directors for guidance. To some degree the concept made sense, but often the advice she got was too conservative for her liking. Make no mistake, Ingrid is no maverick; it's just that she knows herself best and knows that she's at her best when she's in control of her own destiny.

The downside, of course, was that the world wasn't waiting to embrace another recently graduated, nascent practitioner. And if she didn't make a living within nine months or so, she would resent her failing as much as her need for independence, making things potentially worse. Although there was no need to make the decision hastily, this seemed as natural a time as any for a transition and it felt right in terms of justifying a move to begin her own consulting business (having just graduated).

Ingrid did make the move to strike out on her own. It wasn't easy and she didn't make a decent living within her required time period. However, at that point the stakes were too high and she had already made a big investment of both time and money. Because forfeiting it all at that point was really not an option, she made other lifestyle changes and made ends meet until she realized her ultimate success some two years later.

Ingrid has an independent spirit. She made the move to be economically independent, even though it was clearly a more difficult path for her to take. Perhaps we can all learn a lesson from Ingrid: Being independent doesn't always mean being right, but it does mean acting by yourself to accomplish your goals. ◄

Some well-known personalities who seem to exhibit independence include Albert Einstein, Golda Meir, and Frank Lloyd Wright. When speaking with independent people, you're likely to hear phrases like: "We can't be so worried about what others think about us that it inhibits us from doing what we know is right!" or "If we wait for direction, we'll never get anything done."

Inner-Directedness at Work

"Any coward can fight a battle when he's sure of winning; but give me the man who has the pluck to fight when he's sure of losing. That's my way, sir; and there are many victories worse than a defeat.

George Eliot, Janet's Repertoire

▶ A STORY OF INNER-DIRECTEDNESS

The incoming flight was so late that the military personnel and their families had all missed their connections. The stop in Germany was supposed to be just a transition point between the military and civilian airports, but the scheduled bus from the motor pool was nowhere in sight. After having received word that the bus wasn't returning, everybody was told to make his or her own way to a hotel to spend the night. Most were hungry, frustrated, anxious to get home, and in need of a few German marks for the cab fare.

Sergeant Ivan was not happy. His wife and infant son, who were hungry and frustrated as well, accompanied him. Just as others were beginning to resign themselves to making their own way, Sergeant Ivan asked the group to hold on as he made a quick call. Identifying himself only as Ivan, he telephoned the motor pool and asked for the person in charge. After a brief exchange, Ivan simply stated that he was going to collect all of the taxi fare receipts from the group and have them collectively presented to the motor pool for reimbursement, since no bus was being made available at the time to transport the group to a hotel for the night.

The bus from the motor pool arrived within twenty minutes. As all twenty-three soldiers and their families boarded the bus to be taken to the hotel, the driver apologized for the mix-up. Everybody was grateful they didn't have to fend for themselves in a foreign country, late at night, and in need of host currency. All that remained before the bus could depart was the signature from "Captain Ivan" to sign for the authorized transportation.

The moral of the story is that, when Sergeant Ivan's inner voice told him something wasn't right, he took the chance to push back and make it right. Although not a commissioned officer with the authority to sign for the transportation, his inner-directness led him to do the right thing. He knew the motor pool was responsible for getting them to the hotel and he was going to make sure it happened! ◀

Some well-known personalities who seem to exhibit independence include Susan B. Anthony, Martin Luther, and Ben Franklin. When speaking with inner-directed people, you're likely to hear phrases like: "I know in my heart what's right and it's important for me to do this, if only just for myself" or "I'm not afraid to take the road less traveled."

Uniqueness at Work

"One way to change context, Csikszentmihalyi observes, is to position yourself at the intersection of different cultures or disciplines: where beliefs, lifestyles, and knowledge mingle and allow individuals to see new combinations of ideas with greater ease."

Richard Foster and Sarah Kaplan, Creative Destruction

▶ A STORY OF UNIQUENESS

Brenda had never really shrunk away from a good challenge. Throughout her career, she had been known for getting the job done, regardless of circumstances. Her new assignment was taking her overseas, and that meant myriad new possibilities.

Brenda was a strong operations manager. Her leadership and team-building skills helped her pull together diverse production teams. She met or exceeded virtually all of her operations goals. However, Brenda had never been in a minority class herself in terms of ethnic heritage at the workplace. Newly assigned and being transferred to the Japanese division meant even more challenges for Brenda, as she had only a few months to pick up the basics of the language. Further, the Japanese division had strong work units whose bonds transcended the workplace.

Frustrated in her inability to grasp the kana and Chinese characters that made up the Japanese language quickly, Brenda found herself discouraged. She also knew that her transfer was the result of her predecessor having failed in the position after an eighteen-month tenure. Her fears quickly mounted as she began to hear horror stories of loneliness, isolation, and living conditions that were remarkably different from what she had known in the United States.

Nevertheless, Brenda took the assignment with the attitude that she could learn and benefit from the experience. Within the first year, this attitude paid off handsomely for her. She was meeting her production quotas. She worked hard to learn the new language and began to understand how difficult and frustrating it is to adopt new systems, whether learning a new language or changing operating procedures. Occasionally experiencing the requisite faux pas everyone can expect, Brenda actually thrived in her new environment. Learning the language was easier than she had expected once she became steeped in the culture. Her appreciation for her host country's values and norms skyrocketed. Her willingness to learn and grow became a hallmark characteristic her teammates quickly took advantage of.

Brenda's ability to appreciate the uniqueness of her circumstances enabled her to thrive. Her newfound appreciation for teamwork modeled by her hosts went well beyond anything she had previously imagined. Not only was she successful in her assignment, but the experience shaped her leadership skills in a way that no amount of formal learning could. It was by going overseas that Brenda was truly able to arrive as a manager. ◀

Some well-known personalities who seem to exhibit uniqueness include Mother Teresa, Walt Disney, and Gertrude Stein. When speaking with people who value uniqueness, you're likely to hear phrases like: "The beauty of our program is that nobody else is doing it" or "What I like about her is her ability to . . ."

Risk-Taking Driver Stories
Authenticity at Work

"The ultimate measure of a man is not where he stands in moments of comfort and convenience, but where he stands at times of challenge and controversy."

Martin Luther King, Jr.

▶ A STORY OF AUTHENTICITY

Even though Alison was new to the team, she wasn't new to nonprofit organizations. Alison had been holding director-level positions for over fifteen years. Her most recent job change came as a result of an intense recruiting effort by the host organization. Alison hadn't actually been looking for work; this opportunity found her, as so many others had in the past, as a result of her outstanding track record.

At one of her first board meetings, Alison felt uneasy about the way decisions were being made. Everyone seemed to defer to the wishes of the chairperson, seemingly without much candid debate. Demurring to the chairperson was not easy for Alison. Although not necessarily outspoken, she had always voiced her opinions in the past and it seemed to serve her well. The others had to know this about her, as she was a well-known professional who contributed in many ways to the community and its region.

And so she did it; she actually voiced an opposing opinion, much to the chagrin of many of her fellow board members. You could almost hear a collective gasp as she challenged the chairperson and his recommendation to the board. In an instant, the proverbial elephant in the room that had lain dormant for so long had been aroused. Some of the staff members present seemed as wide-eyed as children at a zoo for the first time, virtually staring in disbelief. The anticipated conflict was a scene nobody wanted to miss.

Much to the surprise of everyone, Chairman Johnson reacted in a way that virtually no one anticipated; he thanked Alison for her fresh perspective, and even stated, "What we need around here are a few more good ideas." He actually invited others to chime in and voice their opinions. And as she had so many times before, Alison became the darling of the team for her fearlessness and genuinely authentic ways. ◄

Some well-known personalities who seem to exhibit authenticity include Pope John Paul, George Eliot, and Vladimir Lenin. When speaking with authentic people, you're likely to hear phrases like: "Well, you asked for my opinion" or "It's better to be honest, even though it may hurt others a little."

Resiliency at Work

"The process of living the good life involves an increasing openness to experience. Such openness means an absence of rigidity, of tight organization, of the imposition of structure on experience."

Carl Rogers, On Becoming a Person

▶ A STORY OF RESILIENCY

Randy McFarland was tough. He had to be; as a captain in the merchant marines, he was responsible for a great deal, and much of it often seemed out of control. Randy's story is not unique. It's really quite analogous to most middle managers in corporate America, even though Randy had never been in such an environment.

Randy's office is the command deck of an oceangoing freighter. He leads a team of three officers and twenty-six crew members. His work means crisscrossing the globe some fifty weeks a year. He provides a vital link in making sure that client companies' products reach market—even though he never sees the client and often has freight from multiple clients on each trip. One might intuitively think that "a slow boat from China" could hardly be compared to the fast-paced world of today's demanding corporate climate. Think again.

Captain McFarland has a rigorous job. He is consistently subject to a number of variables beyond his control and yet is no less responsible for delivery of shipments in a timely fashion. Weather, crew shortages, customs inspections, equipment breakdown, language barriers, and an overstressed port authority in many harbors have all contributed to the captain's personal planning philosophy of "hurry up and wait!"

Since so much is often out of his hands, the good captain has to allow for delays in virtually all aspects of his planning. He can no more count on a timely and expedient customs inspection than he can on the weather to cooperate. In most cases his philosophy serves him well. His resiliency is tested on virtually every trip. Caught in the unenviable position of having to deliver product consistently and at the mercy of myriad uncontrollable variables, Captain McFarland has to push hard at every step of the way to stay ahead of schedule and resign himself to eventually falling behind at some point on every trip. It's just the nature of the work.

Clearly, the lesson to be learned here is in realizing that since so much is so often out of our control, we had better develop resiliency. Picking ourselves up and dusting ourselves off after a fall is good. Most of us can do that relatively well when the occasional setback happens. It's how we react to a series of setbacks in succession that is the key to resiliency. Developing this attribute moves us from the reactive, complaining, and victimized mode into a "can do" frame of mind, something many organizations look for in leaders. ◄

Some well-known personalities who seem to exhibit resiliency include Hillary Rodham Clinton, Ted Turner, and Steven Jobs. When speaking with resilient people, you're likely to hear phrases like: "Don't worry about it, we'll figure out a way to make it happen" or "I've been through a lot worse."

Self-Acceptance at Work

"And the wonderful thing about Tiggers [read: Me] is I'm the only one."

A.A. Milne, Winnie-The-Pooh

► A STORY OF SELF-ACCEPTANCE

Sam didn't get the job. This was the second time he was passed over for promotion to national headquarters. The first time was six years ago and he didn't react well then. Sam was being groomed for this position and he didn't want to wait out another administration (which could last ten years!) before getting the opportunity again.

On hearing the news, Sam was distraught. He needed to take inventory. He wanted to figure out the reason he wasn't selected. Was it something about him? Did he do something wrong? What did the other candidate possess that he didn't have? His performance was certainly strong enough at the regional level. "Enough," he thought, "I'm not going to do this to myself. This time is different!'"

Sam quickly came to the realization that it wasn't a matter of figuring out what went wrong. To the contrary, Sam was intent on figuring out what was right. If the organization he worked for didn't see fit to name him the national director, that didn't mean there was something wrong with him. Actually, being a finalist in this situation was quite an honor. After all, is the loser of the national election for President of the United States a failure? Indeed not! So rather than shrink up, Sam decided to get aggressive.

If this wasn't the right opportunity, what was? Many times in life we internalize setbacks as though we've done something wrong. Self-acceptance doesn't mean we forget about self-development activities to shore up our weaknesses. Self-acceptance means liking who you are and where you are in your life's journey. To others, Sam was a remarkable success, a finalist for a national directorship position, clearly a man with a bright future and many opportunities! For Sam to realize this was a giant step forward from the way he reacted the previous time. This time was indeed different! Learning how to become more self-accepting is a lesson many of us could benefit from. ◄

Some well-known personalities who seem to exhibit self-acceptance include Woody Allen, Madonna, and Salvador Dali. When speaking with self-accepting people, you're likely to hear phrases like: "I really feel good about who I am and where I'm going" or "I don't have any regrets!"

The material from this section on drivers is summarized in Table 3.3.

Final Thoughts

As we move further on into the book, we will explore application of the drivers more fully. These drivers of creativity and risk taking are at the heart of every organization's innovative culture. Both the organization's culture and the individuals within it impact its ability to innovate. Learning how to activate the drivers to foster greater creativity and risk taking is what building organizational innovative capacity is about. There are two important ideas that will help in this process. The first is understanding the stop signs to innovation. What gets in our way when we try to move from the left side of the innovation continuum to the right side? Second, we must understand how to connect the need for innovation to the need for concrete results. For this, we must use the four A's: *aim, assess, activate,* and *apply.*

First, however, we're going to take a brief detour and look at innovation from the perspectives of a fairy tale and a contemporary story. These stories may stretch your creative reach. We provide the lessons learned from an age-old parable and invite you to interpret the lessons from a contemporary story. This process will help you gain a clearer perspective on the drivers we discussed in this chapter. For those among you who are driven by practicality and who are looking for swift implementation and action items, skip the next chapter and go right to Chapter 5.

Table 3.3. Driver Reference Sheet

				The Drivers			
	Ambiguity	**Independence**	**Inner-Directed**	**Uniqueness**	**Authenticity**	**Resiliency**	**Self-Acceptance**
Innovation Equation Definitions	Able to operate with uncertainty and vagueness; don't require highly structured organizations, goals, or objectives to accomplish or create	Not subject to the control or influence or determination of another or others; will not subordinate themselves; don't like to be managed	Determine their own expectations and norms; march to the beat of their own drummer	Appreciate and value differences; value uniqueness in both self and others	Being what you purport to be: genuine—"walk your talk," "tell it like it is"	The capacity to spring back, rebound, and successfully adapt and learn, even in the face of adversity and stress	Approving and/or satisfied with your behaviors or actions—"like yourself"
The *American Heritage Dictionary* definition (just for a comparison)	Doubtfulness or uncertainty as regards interpretation: *"leading a life of alleged moral ambiguity"* (Anatole Broyard)	Free from the influence, guidance, or control of another or others; self-reliant: *an independent mind*	Guided in thought and behavior by one's own set of values rather than societal standards or norms	Being the only one of its kind. Without an equal or equivalent; unparalleled	Conforming to fact and therefore worthy of trust. Having a claimed and verifiable origin or authorship. Not counterfeit	The ability to recover quickly from illness, change, or misfortune: buoyancy	Favorable reception; approval
Descriptors	Obscurity, vagueness, indefiniteness	Free, sovereign, autonomous, self-sufficient	OK alone, self-directed, self-reliant, purposeful	Incomparable, peerless, paragon, unmatched	Original, genuine, real, valid, credible, true	Spring, bounce, flexibility, keep on, persevering	Agreement, acquiescence, favor, approval
Well-known personalities	Bill Clinton, Jack Welch, Ehud Barak	Albert Einstein, Golda Meir, Frank Lloyd Wright	Michael Dell, Martin Luther, Ben Franklin	Mother Teresa, Walt Disney, Gertrude Stein	The Pope, George Eliot, Vladimir Lenin	Hillary Rodham Clinton, Ted Turner, Steven Jobs	Woody Allen, Madonna, Salvador Dali

The Drivers

	Ambiguity	Independence	Inner-Directed	Uniqueness	Authenticity	Resiliency	Self-Acceptance
Examples of statements this type of person may make	"Hindsight is always 20/20. Let's just do the best we can with the information we have."	"We can't be so worried about what others think about us that it inhibits us from doing what we know is right!"	"I know in my heart what's right and it's important for me to do this—for myself."	"The beauty of our program is that nobody else is doing it." "What I like about her is her ability to. . . ."	"Well, you asked for my opinion." "It's better to be honest, even if it hurts others."	"Don't worry about that, we'll figure out a way to make it." "I've been through a lot worse."	"I feel good about where I'm going." "I don't have any regrets!"
Descriptors of people who exhibit these drivers	Are OK with disorder. Get upset with too much order around them, feel constrained. Believe that ambiguity is part of the creative process.	Don't like to work for anyone. Don't have to be given direction. Don't ask for help. Believe that their way is the best way.	Believe that no one "really" understands them. March to the beat of their own drummer. Believe that they are responsible for determining their own destiny.	Value creativity in themselves and others. See differences in others; look for differences in others over similarities. Value inventors.	You may not like what they say—but you always know what their opinion is. Walk their talk—what they say is what they do. Are true to themselves.	Get knocked down and get back up again. Always take away something from experiences. Create options; don't get stuck—there's always a way out.	Forgive themselves their mistakes—often have trouble saying, "I'm sorry," because they are OK with their mistakes. Don't have to be perfect.

Ideas for the Consultant

If working with teams or setting the stage for work with an entire organization:

- Show a large version of the Innovative Capacity Continuum and talk about both sides of the continuum.

- Define each driver to develop a shared understanding.

- Have people break into groups and assign them one or two of the drivers to discuss. Have them focus on their team or organization.

- Hand out colored dots and have participants place a dot on each driver continuum. Once all the dots are on the continuum, debrief by asking the team why they put the dot in that location.

  Was there immediate agreement within the group? How does the team/ organization actually exhibit the driver?

  Does the larger group agree/disagree?

- You can also have them place colored dots individually and then talk about the differences. If it is not an intact team, have everyone choose for an organization or team they work for.

- Provide examples of people who exhibit the various drivers.

- Review the Driver Quick-Check with the group and discuss the results either as a large group or in pairs.

- Have participants select personal drivers that they know get in the way of their being more innovative and work in small groups to talk about what they can do to overcome the obstacles to their success.

- Use the Investing in Innovation simulation (Appendix A) to illustrate the drivers at work.

4

Two Tales of Innovation

"When I examine myself and my methods of thought, I come to the conclusion that the gift of fantasy has meant more to me than my talent for absorbing positive knowledge."

Albert Einstein

A Grimms' Fairy Tale
How Six Made Their Way in the World*

Once upon a time there was a man who had mastered all kinds of skills. He had fought in a war and had conducted himself correctly and courageously, but when the war was over, he was discharged and received three pennies for traveling expenses.

"Just you wait!" he said. "I won't put up with that. If I find the right people, I'll force the king to turn over all the treasures of his kingdom to me." Full of rage, he

---

*From THE COMPLETE FAIRY TALES OF THE BROTHERS GRIMM by Jack Zipes, Translator, copyright © 1987 by Jack Zipes. Used by permission of Bantam Books, a division of Random House, Inc.

went into the forest, and there he saw a man tearing up six trees as if they were blades of wheat. "Will you be my servant and travel with me?" he asked. "Yes," the man answered. "But first I want to bring this little bundle of firewood home to my mother." He took one of the trees and wrapped it around the others, lifted the bundle onto his shoulders, and carried it away. Then he returned and went off with the master, who said, "We two shall certainly make our way anywhere in the world."

After they had walked for a while, they found a huntsman who was kneeling down and taking aim at something with a gun. "Huntsman, what are you going to shoot?" the master asked him. "There's a fly sitting on the branch of an oak tree two miles from here. I want to shoot out his left eye," he answered. "Oh, come with me," said the man. "If we three stick together, we'll certainly make our way anywhere in the world." The huntsman was willing and went with him.

As they approached seven windmills, they saw the sails rotating swiftly, even though there was no wind coming from any direction nor was there a leaf stirring. "What in the world can be driving those windmills? There's not a breeze around," the man said. He continued on with his servants for about two miles, and then they saw a man sitting on a tree. He was holding one nostril closed while blowing through the other. "My goodness! What are you doing up there?" the man asked. "Two miles from here are seven windmills," he said "I'm blowing them so that they'll turn." "Oh, come with me," said the man. "If we four stick together, we'll certainly make our way anywhere in the world." So the blower got down from the tree and went along with them.

After some time they saw a man standing on one leg, while the other was lying unbuckled on the ground next to him. "You've made things comfortable for yourself," said the man. "Time for a rest, I suppose?" "I'm a runner," he answered, "and I've unbuckled my leg so that I don't run too fast. When I run with two legs, I go faster than any bird can fly."

"Oh, come with me. If we five stick together, we certainly shall make our way anywhere in the world." So he went along with them, too.

Shortly thereafter they met a man who was wearing a cap that completely covered one of his ears. "Where are your manners?" the master asked him. "You shouldn't drape your cap over one ear like that. You look like a dunce." "It's got to be this way," said the man. "If I put on my cap straight, then a tremendous frost will come and all the birds in the air will freeze and drop dead to the ground."

"Oh, come with me," said the master. "If we stick together, we'll certainly make our way anywhere in the world."

Now the six came to a city where the king had proclaimed that whoever ran a race against his daughter and won would become her husband. But whoever lost would have to pay for it with his head. The man appeared before the king and said, "I want to race but under the condition that one of my servants runs for me." The king answered, "Then his life must also be placed at stake, and you and he will forfeit your lives if you lose."

When they agreed on the terms and everything was set, the master buckled on the runner's other leg and said to him, "Now show us how quick you are and help us win." The runner and the king's daughter were both given jugs and set off running at the same time. Yet, within seconds after the king's daughter had run but a short stretch, the spectators could no longer see the runner, for he soared by them just like the wind. In a short time he arrived at the spring, filled the jug with water, and turned around. Halfway back, however, he was overcome by fatigue, put the jug on the ground, lay down, and fell asleep. For his pillow he had taken a dead horse's skull that had been lying on the ground so that he would not be too comfortable and would wake up in time to continue the race.

In the meantime, the king's daughter, who was much better at running than ordinary people, had reached the spring and was hurrying back with her jug full of water. When she saw the runner lying asleep on the ground, she was delighted and said, "Now the enemy's been delivered into my hands." She emptied his jug and continued running. Everything would have been lost for the runner if the huntsman had not by chance been standing on the top of the castle and if he had not seen everything with his sharp eyes.

"I'll make sure that the king's daughter does not defeat us!" he said, and he loaded his gun and aimed so carefully that he shot the horse's skull from under the runner's head without hurting him. The runner awoke, jumped up, and saw that his jug was empty and that the king's daughter was way ahead of him. However, he did not lose heart, but ran back to the spring with the jug, filled it anew with water, and managed to beat the king's daughter home with ten minutes to spare. "You see," he said, "it was about time that I really started using my legs. I wouldn't exactly call that running, what I was doing before."

However, the king was vexed, and his daughter even more so, that a common discharged soldier should win the race. Therefore, they consulted with each other, seeking a way to get rid of him and all his companions as well. Finally, the king said to her, "I've got an idea. Don't fret. They'll never show their faces around here again."

Then he went to the six and said, "I want you to eat, drink, and be merry." And he led them to a room that had an iron floor. The doors were also made of iron, and the windows were lined with iron bars. In the room there was a table covered with delicious food, and the king said to them, "Go inside and enjoy yourselves."

When they were inside, the king had the door locked and bolted. Then he summoned the cook and commanded him to make a fire and keep it going under the room until the iron became burning hot. The cook did that, and it began to get hot in the room. As the heat became greater and greater, the six wanted to leave the room, but they found the doors and windows locked. They realized that the king meant to suffocate them.

"He won't succeed!" said the man with the cap. "I'm going to let a frost come that will put the fire to shame and send it crawling away." So he put his cap on straight, and immediately there was a frost causing all the heat to disappear and the food on the table to freeze.

After two hours had passed and the king thought they had all perished in the heat, he had the door opened and looked in to see how they were. Yet, when the door was opened, all six of them were well and vigorous; indeed they declared that it would be nice to get outside and warm themselves, for the food had frozen to the dishes because of the cold. The king stormed furiously down the stairs, scolded the cook, and asked him why he had not done what he had ordered. But the cook answered, "There was more than enough heat. Just look for yourself."

The king saw a tremendous fire blazing under the iron room and realized that he could not get the better of the six by doing something like that. So he tried to think of something new to get rid of the unwelcome guests. He summoned the master and said, "If you will accept gold and give up your claim to my daughter, you can take away as much gold as you like."

"That's fine with me, Your Majesty," he answered. "If you give me as much as my servant can carry, I won't claim your daughter." The king was satisfied with that, and the master added, "In two weeks I shall return here to fetch the gold." Then he summoned all the tailors in the entire kingdom, and for two weeks they had to sit and sew a sack. When it was finished, the strong man, who could tear up trees, swung the sack over his shoulder and went to the king, who said, "Who's that powerful fellow carrying such a bundle of canvas on his shoulder? Why, it's as big as a house!" Suddenly he became horrified and thought, "What a lot of gold he'll carry away!" So the king ordered that a ton of gold be brought; this took sixteen of his strongest men to carry; the strong man grabbed it with one hand, put it into the sack, and said, "Why don't you bring more right away? This will barely cover the bottom."

Gradually, the king had his whole treasure brought, and the strong man tossed it all into the sack, but it only became half full. "Bring some more!" the strong man cried. "These few crumbs aren't enough to fill it." So, seventeen thousand wagons of gold from all over the kingdom had to be driven to the spot, and the strong man stuffed them all into the sack, along with the oxen that were harnessed to the wagons.

"Since I don't have the time to inspect everything," he said, "I'll just take what comes until the sack is completely full." When everything was in the sack, there was still room for a lot more, but the strong man said, "I think it's time to put an end to this. Sometimes one has to tie up a sack even if it's not quite full." Then he hoisted it onto his back and went away with his companions.

When the king saw one single man carrying away all the treasures of his kingdom, he was furious and ordered his cavalry to pursue the six and take the sack away from the strong man. Two of the king's regiments soon caught up with the six and called to them, "You're our prisoners! Put down the sack with the gold or else you'll be cut to pieces!"

"What did you say?" asked the blower. "We're your prisoners? Before that ever happens, a lot of you will soon be dancing around in the air." With that he held one nostril and blew through the other at the two regiments, sending them flying in every which direction, up into the blue and over hill and dale. Some were scattered this way, others that way, while a sergeant begged for mercy. Since he was a brave fellow, the blower let up a bit, and the sergeant came out of it without being harmed. Then the blower said to him, "Now go home to the king and tell him that all he has to do is send a few more regiments and I'll blow them all sky high!" When the king received the message, he said, "Let those fellows go. There's something extraordinary about them."

So the six brought their wealth back home, divided it among themselves, and lived happily until their deaths.

Our Interpretation of that Tale

How about that leader? This was truly an *ambiguous* situation; the man had no idea where he was going and how he was going to tackle the situation at the outset. He had a vision, albeit rather negative to start with, but it became positive and his

driving force. And he didn't shy away from being *authentic,* either. He knew what
he wanted and went after it. Along the way, the man found five other men to come
with him (it would have been nice if there had been a few women on this trip, but
remember this tale was written before women existed much as literary heroines)—
men in whom he saw *uniqueness.* He valued their uniqueness and they valued their
own uniqueness and one another's; at least that's what is implied. Their uniqueness may seem quite unusual to the contemporary reader, a hat on sideways to prevent frost? But we can think of a few creative ideas that have presented themselves
at times that people might have considered as peculiar. The fax machine could be
one; data rather than voice traveling through the air waves?

As the story continues, we realize that each man marched to his own drummer;
they were *inner-directed.* They'd been working alone and when an opportunity presented itself for greater benefit, Why not! It made sense to them. They took the risk
to go with a perfect stranger. That may be the ultimate risk; they were giving up
their current situations for what? They didn't know what they were walking into,
but they took the risk. Why? Because they thought that the future benefits out-
weighed their current situation? Did they know for sure? Of course if you knew
what would happen in such a situation, it wouldn't be a risk.

Now remember that they challenged the king's daughter to a race. The leader
and the runner could have both lost their lives. But rather than dwell on the potential losses, they bet on themselves; they bet on one another's unique contributions.
How could they be sure they'd win? They couldn't. Again, that's the risk they were
willing to take. They used their own creativity in a new situation and applied it in
new ways. And wasn't it interesting that when they were in the throes of each challenge the king laid at their feet, they were able to be both *resilient*—bounce back
and figure out a new angle—as well as act *independently.* The huntsman didn't ask
for permission to shoot the skull out from under the runner's head; he saw what
needed to be done and did it. The man with the cap didn't ask for or need permission to keep the locked room cold rather than allowing them to burn alive; he took
the risk. And when the runner made the mistake of falling asleep, he didn't get bent
out of shape and thrash himself for not being "on alert." He was *self-accepting,* doing
just what he had to do. He got up, got some water, and headed off. He didn't wal-
low in the mistake. Put it all together. These guys took their own creativity and
tapped into it in new and different ways to solve new problems. They had to take
risks to be successful and, in so doing, they were not only successful in their pur-

suit, but they were innovative in achieving that success. They increased their own innovative capacity, and at the same time they increased the innovative capacity of the team. What a story of creativity, risk taking, and innovation! The next story is more of what we're likely to experience, but not too far from the lessons learned from this ancient tale!

A Contemporary Story
How Six Made Their Way in the Organization

Once upon a time there was a company named OOPS. This company had barely been making it. For years it would experience ups and downs; some people equated working at OOPS to being on a roller coaster. Whenever there was a decline in revenues, the immediate reaction of leadership was to cut: cut programs, cut staff, cut costs, and cut anything! It seemed they went through these cycles every few years, and just when they thought they'd turned the corner, a new wrinkle in the marketplace brought them full circle again. They'd gotten so used to it that people just expected to take cuts in salaries or be laid off for a period of time.

One day the company was sold and new leadership was installed, something that had not happened in many years. It was at a time when everyone expected layoffs, downsizing, and cuts in salary, but they didn't come. What did come was an all-staff meeting, something quite rare in the history of OOPS. The new president laid out her new objectives. She was going to take the battle into the marketplace rather than to her employees, and she expected everyone to come with her. If they weren't able to commit to her vision of what needed to happen, then they should consider moving on or coming up with another idea, fast. She explained, "We only have a short time to turn this operation around, and if we can do it, then we'll all have jobs and we'll know that we can 'get it done' as individuals and collectively as a company."

Now the new leader was not naïve. She knew that some people were probably going to go back to their offices and grumble about the new direction. These are the "nest soilers." She also knew that some would be extremely excited, and that still more, who represented the majority, would make a statement like, "We'll just wait and see." She had decided before even presenting her game plan that she was going to depend on her own leadership team and those who were with her to drive the company forward. And although she'd met with the leadership team several times to get their buy-in in the last few weeks, she felt as though some people were on the sidelines waiting to say, "We told you it wouldn't work!" This was unacceptable and she intended to find out who was committed to the cause and who was not.

She stopped into the CFO's office and asked him whether he was on board and what he thought he and his staff could do in terms of helping out. This was a good question because it put the onus on the CFO. She wanted to see whether he'd been thinking about where they needed to go or whether he was one of those "wait and see" people. Indeed, the CFO had been thinking along the same lines as the new president and he was ready with a few good ideas. He said that he had some discretionary resources to do some in-depth analysis and financial modeling that might present the business in such a way that everyone could get a handle on the current situation or see the business differently, including how their individual and team actions could help the company move swiftly to combat its challenges. These were some of the things that the previous leadership hadn't been interested in trying. The CFO was very excited about this idea, and the president was pleased.

Then she went to see the vice president of marketing and sales. He was used to being harassed to produce miraculous sales results when downturns like this occurred. But instead of harassing him, the president just asked a bunch of questions, probing to find out when sales were strongest, which product lines were marginal, which lines had promise, and about alternative selling strategies. As the president knew the CFO could offer some help in terms of resources, she suggested that the two executives meet to do some quick work.

Next she stopped at the door of the VP of operations and asked her if she was ready to get on board. The VP was cynical. She had seen this type of thing before. But she felt that if she didn't give it a chance and show a positive face that she'd merely be labeled a naysayer. She went on to say that her strength was in building teams of the different business functions, especially the cross-functional type teams that she thought they needed right now. Although she was not enamored with the thought of losing more of her staff, especially in the purchasing department, where they had made some great progress in improving supplier delivery times, she reluctantly agreed to meet with the CFO to review what she thought would be some painful scenarios.

As the president went a little farther down the hallway, she stopped into the office of the vice president of human resources. He looked a little glum and so she asked him if it was something to do with the new strategic direction. Much to the president's surprise, he said, "Absolutely not! If we don't take the risk now, we'll run the chance of losing the company and everyone loses in that case. I have some ideas for how to provide incentives to some of our people that just might tip the scales in our favor. And I have a few ideas on training programs that were shelved in the last downturn that could really generate some excitement as well as help us toward making some substantial productivity gains. We've got to get some new ideas flowing and take some chances to make it happen. I'll have some stuff for you to review by the end of the week. This whole idea of getting people to work more cross-functionally will no doubt raise some eyebrows, so I want to be ready with some positive messages and incentives to make it successful."

The president was a little bit shocked and yet pleasantly surprised at how her executive team was responding.

And with that, she turned the corner and knocked on the door of the head of R&D. "Well, what do you think?" she asked. "Are we on the right track?" He replied that, although he had some concerns, this downturn in business afforded him the opportunity to realign his people. He then went on to comment that he had some ideas for streamlining production. "It may cost some money up-front, but it should make us more efficient, increase our capacity, and help get us back in the game. We haven't invested in any new technology for a long time, and I've been researching several processes that could really make a big difference." The president struggled for a moment with the idea of spending more money and then reluctantly agreed to give him the green light and try his solutions. She knew that taking the risks to innovate sometimes required doing things that initially seemed counterintuitive.

As it turned out, an interim analysis that the accounting department conducted uncovered the fact that one of the newly acquired product lines that had initially shown promise had sales that slowed to a trickle. The sales group responded to the situation relatively quickly by getting together with the marketing group to discuss why the launch had floundered. After further investigation, together they realized that the product had required more customer service than expected. However, product margins were high enough to absorb some additional costs. Therefore, moving the freed-up expeditors in purchasing to customer service, coupled with an aggressive new sales campaign, had the potential to grow sales dramatically. And just like that it was done!

Over the next six months, every one of the OOPS leaders worked together to make the company more successful; to everyone's disappointment, more and more challenges came from right and left. The operations people balked at the new financial modeling, many employees reacted negatively to the cross-functional training, and the incentives programs were met with reservation, if not outright skepticism. It seemed like at every turn the leadership team was running into resistance.

However, the leadership team hung together. Gradually they started to see people come on board. Soon thereafter they started to achieve some successes. They were driving the vision together, creatively solving problems, and taking some reasonable risks for the first time in the history of the organization. Oh sure, not everything worked. In fact, it seemed like things got much worse initially. But then customers began to see the kind of service that they needed, and they rewarded the company with increased orders. The new manufacturing technologies that they adopted were lightening the load for the production workers, and it seemed like everyone had more time to create solutions and prevent problems from arising rather than just reacting to the issues of the day. The vice president of operations reported that by streamlining manufacturing, inventory turnover had increased and that by single-sourcing suppliers across the company, the company was saving not only time and money, but was getting higher quality and dealing with fewer vendors.

New ideas were starting to flow. People felt more and more comfortable offering ideas. Creativity and risk taking were starting to become an integral part of who they were as a company. They became successful, innovative, and glad to know that, when the chips were down, they could rely on themselves.

Right before the end of the second quarter, the president called an all-staff meeting to congratulate everyone for their hard work. She emphasized that by working creatively to solve problems and taking a few chances, they had effectively turned the company around. They toasted their success with champagne and ate a little cake too. Further, she reminded them not to lose track of their future or forget what worked to get them this far. "And now, I'd like to propose that we rename the company from OOPS to AAAH. What do you think?" Everyone just looked at each other and sighed a collective groan.

Your Interpretation of that Tale

Take a few moments and reflect on this story. Think about how each person approached the problems. What was their innovation orientation? What drivers were operating? Use the space provided below to jot down your interpretation of the lesson.

These examples help illustrate how people approach challenges they're often faced with. Think about stories from your own organization. How do these stories unfold? Are there any examples of creativity and risk taking? What are some of the stop signs inhibiting your organization's innovative efforts? In the next chapter we explore the nature of these stop signs.

Ideas for the Consultant

If working with teams or setting the stage for working with an entire organization:

- Have the participants talk about the Grimms' fairy tale. Which character did they like most? Why?

- Have everyone share his or her own interpretation of the contemporary story. Break the group into pairs or small groups for discussion. Is the story real? What are some things that could have potentially changed the way the story played out? Could they have done anything differently at OOPS?

- Have people write their own fairy tale or contemporary story and discuss it.

---

(5)

The Stop Signs to Innovation

"Let us not look back in anger, or forward with fear, but around in awareness."

James Thurber

WHETHER IN OEDIPUS' CASE with the Sphinx blocking his passage with a conundrum, a middle manager impairing a career, or finding our way through the maze of daily life to make ourselves heard, we are all faced with impediments that prevent us from being as creative and taking the risks to be more innovative. Most of the impediments (or whether you want to call them stop signs or, as some people call them, dragons, gremlins, or monsters) blocking our path to success in these two important areas are most often the result of our own fears and the messages we send ourselves. And the things we most want to have happen, the innovations we want to see, are halted in their tracks. However, recognizing and learning how to deal with our stop signs, dragons, gremlins, or monsters is what this chapter is all about. For simplicity, let's stick to the more concrete language of stop signs, but be creative and substitute another word if one fits better for you.

Take a moment and recall the riddle of the Sphinx. If you don't recall it, let us remind you of that ancient Greek story that holds so many messages for today.

"Lonely and homeless, Oedipus arrived at Thebes in Greece, which was beset by a dreadful monster called the Sphinx. The frightful creature frequented the roads to the city, killing and devouring all travelers who could not answer the riddle that she put to them. The riddle was, what walks on four legs in the morning, on two legs at noon, and on three legs in the evening? The answer was man [today we'd say human being], who in infancy crawls on all fours, in adulthood walks upright on two legs, and in old age uses a cane. When Oedipus solved her riddle, the Sphinx killed herself."

The idea is that we can all be overwhelmed by our fears and it often takes understanding and one simple word to destroy that which we are most fearful of and make it disappear.

Stop Signs to Innovation

Frequently, organizational leaders question why there aren't more innovative efforts or innovations floating to the top. We hear executives state things like, "We value creativity and innovation around here. It's even written into our mission statement!" Yet declaring the need for something rarely means it's going to happen.

Sometimes the reality of our environment doesn't line up with the espoused values. We've all heard the remarks, "It doesn't matter if you make a mistake. We all make mistakes. What matters is that we learn from them." However, the reality is that in many instances when someone in an organization makes a mistake, he or she is criticized or held up as an example of what not to do. We all know that making mistakes often costs the organization money, clients, goodwill, competitive advantage, and so forth. This phenomenon of saying one thing and acting another way is what we call "espoused exposure." This is a situation where the subsequent resulting actions (or threats) speak louder than the words (or espoused values), thereby leaving the embraced value exposed to harsh criticism. The result is that it doesn't really matter what is said because the reality of the situation is different.

Other times, the organization's leaders assume they know what's important, while employees hold different beliefs. Consider the research cited by Boone and Kurtz (1982), wherein managers and workers ranked the importance of various morale factors. Management held the view that good wages and job security were most important, whereas employees ranked full appreciation for work well done and feeling "in" on things as most important. These incongruent beliefs affect organizational effectiveness.

The ramifications for such egregious misperceptions are profound. If organization leaders hold one set of assumptions while employees hold another, by definition the resulting dichotomy thwarts efforts to move the organization forward efficiently. For example, if management holds money as most important in terms of what employees want, they are likely to motivate employees and design incentive systems to reward behaviors consistent with this paradigm. Conversely, if the value the employees place on management's programs is low because what they desire most is satisfying the esteem need of feeling appreciated, the resulting contributions are marginalized.

Similarly, in terms of innovation, unresolved conflicting values, either espoused or tacit, have the same result. Consider the following example. An electronics manufacturer in a price-sensitive market segment consistently positions itself as a cost-competitive producer. Further, to maintain its competitive edge, it must regularly introduce new features and occasionally new products. The resulting edict to employees is to innovate efficiently. Personnel in the company's R&D department have numerous alternative opportunities. Intuitively, they have a good idea of which innovations might best serve the company. Unfortunately, most product innovations are rarely cost competitive when first introduced. Therefore, efforts are concentrated in areas that are only the most cost-efficient. Again, we see the resulting contributions marginalized. The competing values framework (Quinn, Hildebrandt, Rogers, & Thompson, 1991) thoroughly examines different dimensions of managerial communication that are opposite or competing values. The model takes into account a multidimensional approach whereby strength in one dimension may directly cause weakness in another (Stevens, 1996).

These phenomena occur in organizations today at both the macro and micro levels. Individuals, departments, cross-functional work teams, and whole organizations fall prey to these conflicting values. The signals of innovative inhibitions are similar at any level.

We have identified the frequent stop signs that often inhibit innovative efforts. Ask yourself or your organization whether you need to _____ (fill in the blank from the left-hand column of Table 5.1). If the answer is yes, then odds are you're stifling the corresponding driver (listed in the right-hand column).

Table 5.1. The Stop Signs to Innovation

The Stop Signs (I/We need to)	The Driver
Always be informed Have all the answers Be logical/rational Be prepared for anything	Ambiguity
Go through channels Do it (work) with others Check in with others Be a team player all the time	Independence
Be liked Impress others Be responsible for others Trust, obey others	Inner-Directed
Be on time Be consistent Conform Look and dress the part	Uniqueness
Protect our turf Guard against attacks Lobby my/our interests Develop alliances	Authenticity
Finish it Win at all costs Produce—get results Be able to take it	Resiliency
Be right Prove myself Earn the right to play Be worthy	Self-Acceptance

The more the drivers of creativity and risk taking are inhibited by these stop signs, the less likely you'll be able to accelerate your innovative capacity.

The stop signs are not necessarily unique to each driver. Often individual stop signs will apply to more than one. For example, having to "go through channels" may affect your ability to accept ambiguity, operate independently, or be authentic. Try some of them on and see just how they come into play for yourself, others around you, and the organizations and teams you work with and for. Some of these stop signs are carried throughout the organization and become the modus operandi of an organization, preventing creativity and risk taking from occurring at all levels.

Illustrating the Power of the Stop Signs

In this section, we'll use an example of a statement from each of the seven drivers and illustrate the power of a stop sign to restrict innovation. We use dialogue to illustrate the power of understanding drivers and the stop signs in the conversation.

A series of driver challenges follows each dialogue. They are organized to introduce the drivers first in a broad way, followed by observing others wrestling with them, then personalizing the drivers and going in-depth with them in specific situations.

1. Broad Challenge—providing a conceptual (more academic) understanding of the driver;

2. Observational Challenge—watching the driver in action and beginning to internalize it;

3. Personal Challenge—internalizing the driver and understanding it at a personal level; and

4. In-Depth Challenge—challenging you to activate the driver in a way that's specific and unique to you.

Stop Sign: The Need to Always Be Informed

This affects our ability to accept ambiguity. It means that we seek predictability. *Example:* Kevin, the CEO, needs continuous updates from regional operating companies.

Kevin   "If you have a few minutes, Bob, I'd like to talk about your quarterly initiatives."

Bob   "Sure, what's up?"

Kevin	"I heard from Larry that you've already started on some of the projects."
Bob	"You bet. I want to make sure I get a good start this quarter."
Kevin	"Well, we hadn't actually talked about each of the initiatives and I'm a little bit concerned if you've started on the Phoenix project."
Bob	"OK. Is there a problem with the Phoenix project?"
Kevin	"Bob, you know we haven't discussed this project and I can't have my regional operating managers all out there spending money on half-baked ideas."
Bob	"This is not a half-baked idea! We've been talking about this off and on for over a year. The time is right. If I don't get started now we'll miss the window of opportunity."
Kevin	"Let's get clear for a moment here. . . ."
Bob	"C'mon, Kevin, if I have to wait to get your approval on all my projects, we'll never meet any of our objectives."
Kevin	"Bob, this is a quarter-million-dollar expenditure. Do you know what will happen if all nine of our regions do this? I have to control our expenditures. For goodness sake, Bob, take a minute. . . ."
Bob	"Kevin, I'm on the same team! Why would I want to. . . ."
Kevin	"Bob . . . Bob, hold on a second here. I'm not saying you can't do the Phoenix project. I'm telling you that we need to talk about it and approve it before we move ahead with it. You have to understand that you need to follow the process we've outlined."
Bob	"But if we go to committee on this it'll just get bogged down."
Kevin	"I'm sorry. But if I make an exception here, then I'm sending the signal that its OK to move ahead without communicating and getting prior approval."
Bob	"C'mon, Kevin. You aren't telling me to stop the project, are you?"
Kevin	"I'm sorry, Bob, but I need some more information before I can give you the nod to move ahead with this."

How might the situation change if Kevin became aware of how his personal need for information is potentially affecting his organization? What might happen if both Bob and Kevin were aware of their own stop signs? While predicting the outcome may be difficult, if both Bob and Kevin were aware of their stops signs, this alone would have changed the dialogue. And when the dialogue changes, the probability for different outcomes changes too.

When trying to develop your tolerance for dealing with *ambiguity*, the following challenges will help.

Broad Challenge. Think of two leaders who have faced a crisis. Contrast the way in which each dealt with the crisis and their comfort level with the ambiguity of the crisis. For example, compare how President Kennedy handled the Bay of Pigs incident with the way President Carter handled the Iran hostage crisis. Which President had to deal with greater levels of ambiguity? How cautious were they in their respective approaches?

Observational Challenge. View the video of *Apollo 13*. Catapulting though space with no power and waiting for Mission Control to offer alternative solutions, you realize you may not be able to reach earth again and there's little you can do. What sustains you? How would you react?

Personal Challenge. Put yourself in a situation at work in which you need to take action without having all of the information. What's the best outcome? The worst?

In-Depth Challenge. Take a walk though the woods. Wander with no destination or time line in mind. Observe the intricacies of the forest. Reflect on the structures (plant, animal, human) or lack thereof. Embrace the ambiguity. Become aware of what feelings stir inside you with such an ill-defined situation and purpose.

Now let's take a look at how another stop sign can adversely affect an organization.

Stop Sign: The Need to Work with Others

This stop sign affects our ability to operate independently. It means we are dependent on others. *Example:* Department heads confer on strategic initiatives.

Melanie	"Hey, Pete, did you get the word on the strategic update?"
Pete	"No, I just got back from New York late last night. Today's my first day back in the office. Did I miss something?"
Melanie	"Did you miss something? You don't have to be out of town to miss something around here!"
Pete	"What's up?"
Melanie	"Well, it's just that we're using the new NoMX software that Bill over in IT developed to roll out the programs in the third quarter."
Pete	"So?"

Melanie	"So . . . you obviously didn't go to the informational session, did you?"
Pete	"No, I didn't. I've been really busy lately."
Melanie	"What a joke. I don't have any confidence in this program! When Sharon was beta testing it last month, she reported at least a half-dozen bugs in the program."
Pete	"Well, maybe they're fixed by now."
Melanie	"Get real. I've already talked to Fred and Stan and they're with me. We're not going to use it. I suggest you think long and hard about it before you decide to use it."

As she stated in her last sentence, Melanie's stop sign is repeating itself in multiple conversations. Will she single-handedly be able to derail the initiative? This phenomenon has occurred in more than one organization. Again, we might wonder how she or Pete might behave differently if they were aware of the driving influences. Even if Melanie isn't capable of policing herself, odds are that both the dialogue and outcomes would be influenced if just one person in the organization recognized the stop sign and called the question.

When trying to develop your ability to operate *independently*, begin by practicing the following challenges:

Broad Challenge. Explore independence from the perspective of Czechoslovakians during the 1968 Soviet takeover. In what ways did they maintain their independence?

Observational Challenge. View the video of the movie *Wall Street*. What internal transformation is happening when the protagonist begins to realize he's been seduced?

Personal Challenge. Recall a situation at work in which you gave in to peer pressure rather than stand up for what you believed in. Explore your emotions during this process. What might have happened had you stood your ground?

In-Depth Challenge. Create your own agenda. That is, write your own to-do list. Prioritize the list and complete it in the order you choose. Reflect on how much credence you give others' priorities. What concerns you about acting independently?

In the next example, we see how even the best of intentions can go awry.

Stop Sign: The Need to Impress Others

This stop sign affects our ability to be inner-directed. It means we become more other-directed. *Example:* Presentation gets out of hand.

Tom   "I can't believe you did that! What were you thinking? You've been through this kind of thing before. Well? We're really going to have to smooth things over with Deb."

Linda   "Take it easy, Tom. There's no need to be melodramatic here."

Tom   "I'm not being melodramatic, Linda! We have a process for these things, and this was not the right time for you to push your personal agenda."

Linda   "Personal agenda? What are you talking about? There's a reason you picked my store for the VIP visit. What was it? C'mon now, the truth."

Tom   "The truth is I should have listened to Jess. She warned me."

Linda   "Warned you? Warned you about what? Let me tell you something, Tom. We're all on the same team here. I was just trying to show that we have ideas here . . . that we can think for ourselves. . .that we don't need to always rely on corporate for everything."

Tom   "Linda, listen to me. There's a time and a place for everything. We don't have the luxury or freedom to just go off and do these kinds of things on our own. I don't care who you were trying to impress. Our franchise license may be in jeopardy."

Linda   "Please, Tom. You make it sound like what I did was criminal. All I did was. . . ."

Tom   "We know, we know. Next time check in with me beforehand. No, better yet, there won't be a next time."

Linda   "Thanks for the vote of confidence, Tom."

Tom is other-directed. Threatened by the impressions his manager leaves, he is quick to chastise Linda for being inner-directed. Many times even the slightest of original expressions are threatening to organizations. Even without knowing the details of Linda's faux pas, we're left to imagine a different scene where Tom, albeit not pleased, is more understanding. Clearly, organizations need parameters for appropriate conduct, but does the need to impress others have to snuff out all individual expression?

When working on becoming more *inner-directed*, the following challenges will help:

Broad Challenge. Examine Jesse "The Body" Ventura's quest to become governor of Minnesota. What was his platform? To what degree was he inner-directed?

Observational Challenge. View the video of the movie *Dead Poets Society.* What value does Professor Keating offer the students that no one else does? To what degree and in what ways are the students becoming inner-directed?

Personal Challenge. List several reasons why you were hired. List the skills and experience you offer the company that no one else does. List several things you can do to make yourself more valuable to the company.

In-Depth Challenge. The next time you're in a group setting and the group decides to take a certain course of action, ask yourself what you would like to do. For example, let's say that at lunch everyone decides to go out for pizza and you'd rather have Mexican, go out to lunch for Mexican all by yourself. How does this feel? Exhilarating? Inappropriate?

In the final example for the creativity drivers, we explore how powerfully the need to conform can inhibit valuing unique contributions.

Stop Sign: The Need to Conform

This stop sign affects our ability to operate uniquely and look for it in others. *Example:* Market research drives R&D awry.

Dan	"There you have it, PJ. On time, and ready to roll."
PJ	"Thanks, Dan. You guys up in marketing always get the data!"
Dan	"What do you mean by that?"
PJ	"By what? I mean, you guys get the data. That's good."
Dan	"The data doesn't lie, PJ. I know you think you know what's best, but we're a company that's driven by the data."
PJ	"Listen, nobody needs to tell me about the value of data. What do you think we do down here in R&D anyway? Sometimes you need to use your head a little and read between the lines."
Dan	"What's your problem anyway?"
PJ	"Dan, let me just say this. Didn't your data say the way to go was to drive our core business units? And while we were doing that, we got

whipped in the spring market rollout. With no new product releases, we just sat there at the national convention with egg on our faces."

Dan   "Now wait a minute, PJ. That wasn't my. . . ."

PJ   "Wait for what? More data?"

Dan   "Hey, you know the way the system works around here. If you've got a problem with the way. . . ."

PJ   "Yeah, yeah, I know. Don't give me any of the 'take it up at the team meeting' stuff. If we don't start thinking with our heads around here, we're going to be in big trouble."

Dan   "Yeah? Like having everyone go off and do their own thing is going to help. Get with the program, PJ. I'll admit the system isn't perfect, but it's all we have; and you don't just get to go off half-cocked. If you've got a problem, work the issue through the proper channels like everyone else does."

PJ   "That's exactly my point! Don't you see? We've got to start shaking things up a bit. There's so much talent here that's being wasted 'cause we all have to 'go through channels.' It's all about. . . ."

Dan   PJ, save it. I've got a ten o'clock and we're not going to solve anything today anyway. You've got our report; I suggest you don't ignore it. See you at the team meeting."

PJ and Dan both want the organization to succeed. However, each has varying degrees of tolerance for recognizing the potential unique contributions of others. Perhaps Dan's need to conform to established protocol at all costs is hiding something? Maybe Dan isn't sure of himself and his abilities. Often people hide behind conforming as a way of dealing with their own inability to appreciate unique contributions. Regardless of cause, Dan would be better suited to draw out some of PJ's thoughts to develop a greater shared understanding. Who knows where this would lead?

When working on our ability to value *uniqueness* in others and ourselves, the following challenges will help:

Broad Challenge. With the advent of cable television and satellites, the number of available viewing channels is growing every day. What value is there in offering seemingly endless television choices? How does it potentially affect the generation of new ideas?

Observational Challenge. View the video of *Toy Story*. What happens to Woody's character when other characters are introduced?

Personal Challenge. It has been said that effective leadership is unique—specific to the individual, like his or her own fingerprint. Name a unique characteristic about how you go about leading others or doing your work.

In-Depth Challenge. Observe closely the uniqueness of individual expressions (for example, clothing, hair style, jewelry, cars, contents of bag lunches, and so on). How do you react? Are you appreciative? Disdainful? How does this attitude manifest itself in your work or other areas of your life?

Now, let's look at the risk-taking drivers.

Stop Sign: The Need to Protect Our Turf

This stop sign affects our ability to act in authentic ways. It means we act politically. *Example:* Examining the unattended consequences of a zero-based budgeting program.

Jennifer	"Jim, I haven't seen your fourth-quarter training requests yet."
Jim	"I know, I know. I'm not sure we going to do much this quarter. We're swamped."
Jennifer	"But you really haven't done much training all year."
Jim	"I know. It's just that we have our hands full with the current rollout."
Jennifer	"You are aware that you're going to lose your whole budget for this next year."
Jim	"Ouch. I forgot about that.
Jennifer	"I can't believe your team doesn't have any training needs."
Jim	"Well, of course we do. The timing just isn't good right now."
Jennifer	"Jim, you might want to think about making some time for it.
Jim	"Or I can just deal with it later too."
Jennifer	"What do you mean?"
Jim	"I'm under budget in a couple of areas this year, so I'll just pad those accounts next year and transfer the money internally. Ed doesn't have time to pay attention to every line item. As long as I'm under budget as a whole, I'll be just fine.
Jennifer	"Do you think that's wise?"

Jim   "It's not about being wise, Jen. It's about navigating the system, play-ing the game. I'll pass on the training for now and talk to you soon. I've got to run. See you later."

Of all the things squandering organization resources today, the biggest culprit is perhaps the political environment or "protecting one's turf." In an ideal situa-tion, Jim might not have to take advantage of Ed's missing the details. When an authentic culture is cultivated, quality conversations begin to move organizations toward their goals.

When working on our *authenticity*, the following challenges will help:

Broad Challenge. Which 20th Century figure has demonstrated the most authen-ticity to you? Why?

Observational Challenge. View the video of *The Hunt for Red October*. What credi-bility issues does the CIA analyst face throughout the film? How does he handle these issues?

Personal Challenge. Do you think people find you genuine? If so, why? If not, specifically list several things you can do to increase your credibility at work.

In-Depth Challenge. Are the words "I disagree" in your vocabulary? How about, "That's your opinion"? The next time you catch yourself thinking these thoughts, take a risk and voice them; go ahead, tell it like it is. Assert your opinions and val-ues. What concerns you about doing this?

The following example illustrates how the need for personal wins can be a detri-ment to the organization.

Stop Sign: The Need to Win

This affects our ability to be resilient. It means we operate with greater rigidity. *Example:* Regional performance results in holding back information.

Rachel   "Wow, Colleen! You're leading the region again in all three categories. Congratulations."

Colleen   "Thanks, I'm just lucky I guess."

Rachel   "Yeah, right. I don't think luck has anything to do with it."

Colleen   "Well, we do have a good team. They know what they're doing. And remember, they do have one of the best leaders! Just kidding."

Rachel	"Don't sell yourself short. You are good. I was hoping that during our next conference call you'd share some of your recent successes so the rest of the country can catch up."
Colleen	"I suppose I could do that."
Rachel	"You don't sound very excited about it. What's going on?"
Colleen	"Um . . . how do I say this? Rachel, can I trust you?"
Rachel	"Where's that coming from? Of course you can trust me!"
Colleen	"I know. It's just that . . . well, I need to come out on top again this quarter, if you know what I mean."
Rachel	"No, I don't, not really. What do you mean?"
Colleen	"Rachel, I'm the only female regional manager, and you know as well as I do that there are no female vice presidents. So therefore, I need to consistently out-perform everyone. It's just the reality of the situation if I ever want to see a promotion."
Rachel	"What about the bigger picture? Everyone knows you're tops, and helping everyone else out is just going to be another feather in your cap."
Colleen	"Eric was the last person promoted, and that was over three years ago. The way I see it, nobody's moving at the top for a long time, except for Jim, and even he has three to five years left. If I don't look out for me, who will?"
Rachel	"C'mon, you don't know that for sure. Things change all the time."
Colleen	"Oh yeah? How long has it been since your last promotion?"
Rachel	"That's different, Colleen. I'm in a staff function."
Colleen	"Well it's no different in operations, Rachel. I'm not saying I won't do it. I'm just saying . . . well, I can't share all my trade secrets."
Rachel	"I don't get it."
Colleen	"Get this: I'm going to be the next vice president, Rachel, and I'm going to do whatever I have to do to make it happen!"

Clearly, Colleen's desire to win means holding back from the organization. Is it possible that Colleen's need to win needn't have to mean this? Surely the organization would be better served if she shared her successes. But what kind of environment would need to be fostered? Not only does Colleen need to be aware of her stop sign, to win, but the organization needs to be aware of the culture that may even encourage such behaviors. Herein we see the need to work the issues on all levels; the individual, team, and organizational.

When working on developing *resiliency*, the following challenges will help:

Broad Challenge. Since its inception in 1948, the state of Israel has been in virtually constant war with its neighboring Arab nations. Examine the resolve and will of the Israeli people throughout its existence. How have they been individually and collectively resilient as a people?

Observational Challenge. View the video of the movie *Working Girl.* How does the main character exhibit resiliency and at what cost?

Personal Challenge. Think about a recent time at work in which there was a setback for you or your team. Explore the emotions associated with the setback. How did you react?

In-Depth Challenge. The next time you have a setback or make a mistake, pay close attention to how you react. How long do you dwell on the issue? What tapes keep playing over and over in your thoughts? Make a conscious effort to bounce back quickly. Introduce a new thought: "I'm over it!" (As in, I'm done grieving about this issue; it's in the past, let's move on).

In the last example, we show how pervasive the stop signs can be; especially when they are driven from the top down.

Stop Sign: The Need to Be Right

This stop sign affects our ability to be self-accepting. It means we tend to become more victimized. *Example:* "Don't challenge me in a meeting," says CEO Matt to key lieutenants.

Matt "Which is why I don't want you to challenge me. Is that clear?"

Jacob "No, it's not. Help me understand this again."

Matt "What part don't you get? We need to present a unified front here. If the committee members think we're questioning ourselves, it creates doubt. They look to me to be a strong visionary, and I can't be that if you guys are challenging me in front of them. I don't mind if you want to talk to me off-line afterwards, but not in front of them. Got it?"

Jacob	"I hear what you're saying, Matt, but for goodness sakes . . . I'm not sure about this. I mean, well . . . we need to wrestle with some of these tough issues. There's a lot of wisdom in the group. We need to take advantage of that."
Matt	"I don't disagree with you. What I'm saying is that when I make a call, that's it. End of story."
Jacob	"But, what if?"
Matt	"But, but nothing, Jacob. If you're not on the same page with me on this, then it may be time for you to take a good hard look at. . . ."
Jacob	"See, Matt, this is what I'm talking about. This type of heavy-handed stuff squelches our ability to get at the heart of what's going on."
Matt	"OK, Jacob, tell me. What's going on? Go ahead, get it off your chest."
Jacob	"Um . . . no, I get it. I see your point, Matt."
Matt	"Anything else then?"
Jacob	"No."
Matt	"Thanks, Jacob. I appreciate your support."

Sometimes the need to be right goes all the way to the top. In this case, Matt is mandating a culture wherein he is never challenged in meetings. Today, many organizations tout the values of teamwork over the leader as hero role. But if the organization's leaders have personal stop signs, they can inhibit an organization from realizing its potential. In many cases, these types of leaders don't mean to inhibit; it's an unintended consequence of personal stop signs. While others may be quick to recognize them, without the framework to begin a dialogue around such issues, it is unlikely organizations will be able to overcome such actions.

When working on becoming more *self-accepting,* the following challenges will help:

Broad Challenge. Oprah Winfrey's struggle with maintaining her desired weight has been widely publicized. What factors might be influencing her desire to lose weight? Why do you suppose there is a cyclical nature to her weight loss?

Observational Challenge. View the video of *Pretty in Pink.* How does the adolescent's struggle with self-acceptance parallel your own struggles with self-acceptance?

Personal Challenge. Examine your relationships with your co-workers. With whom are you friends? Ask them what it is that they like about you. Does it reflect what you like about yourself?

In-Depth Challenge. Think about yourself and all you have to offer. List your strengths and weaknesses on a sheet of paper. Recognize your assets as well as potential liabilities to others; accept them. Quit saying you're sorry. Free yourself from personalizing everything.

The stop signs to innovation are not always clearly marked at organizational intersections. They frequently cause accidental inhibitions when people fail to recognize them. Knowing the power they have to counter efforts in building innovative teams is the first step to reducing their impact. Keep the aforementioned illustrations in mind as you read how to build innovative organizations and teams in the next chapter using the four A's (4As): aim, assess, activate, and apply.

Ideas for the Consultant

If working with teams or setting the stage for work with an entire organization:

- Define what a stop sign looks like for your organization. Act some of the examples out using props.

- Ask the members of the team/organization to share the name that they use for their own stop signs to innovation. Do they use the words fear, gremlin, goblin, or others?

- Have members take the list of stop signs and select one that is associated with the driver they've selected to work on as individuals or teams. This can be done as a group or individually.

- Then have individuals within the group share the driver and the stop sign that they've selected. Pair up or put people into small groups who have similar drivers and stops signs and ask them to discuss how the stop sign is an impediment to moving that driver from the left to the right side of the driver continuum.

- Ask them to also create a challenge that they could begin working on. The challenge can be one of the challenges presented in this chapter or something that they develop themselves.

6

The Innovation
Equation in Action

"Never tell people how to do things. Tell them what to do and they will surprise you with their ingenuity."

George S. Patton

BASED **ON OUR DISCUSSIONS** to this point, what are the practical messages for today's organizations?

- "Thinking out of the box," building a new box, or changing what's in the box can be fostered;
- Risk taking can be developed in organizations, teams, and individuals;
- Creativity can be developed in organizations, teams, and individuals;
- Speed of creativity and risk taking can be enhanced; and
- Innovation is a reality for you, your team, and your organization!

This chapter takes you one step closer to making the kinds of changes required to accelerate innovative capacity. The four A's (4As) for building innovative capacity and implementing the Innovation Equation include:

- Aim
- Assess
- Activate
- Apply

The 4As: Aim, Assess, Activate, Apply

Translating theory to application is the focus to this chapter. It has been our experience as practitioners that sometimes models don't translate well into action. Occasionally minor adjustments are required, while other times the models just don't translate well at all. We kept this in mind as we developed the 4As for implementing the Innovation Equation. The result is a deceptively simple approach that, when applied, yields powerful results.

In brief, the 4As, illustrated in Figure 6.1, start with developing a goal (aim), assessing your current capacity to reach the goal (assess), determining which actions to leverage to help you get there (activate), and then applying them to the original aim (apply) on a daily basis—completing the cyclical and iterative nature of the approach to innovation.

Figure 6.1. The 4As

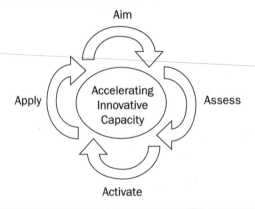

Accelerating Innovative Capacity

In one sense, when we talk about innovative capacity, we are actually talking about accelerating versus building innovative capacity. Literally speaking, we are not building innovation but accelerating our capacity for innovation. The raw materials must exist in order for this to happen. Unlike something that needs construction, the ability to innovate (that is, the ability to create and take risks) lies within each of us.

Releasing the inherent creative and risk-taking drivers within each of us is what we're trying to do, and this is why using the word *accelerating* is an attractive alternative to the word building when talking about increasing innovative capacity. To accelerate means to cause to occur sooner than expected. This is the goal, as well as the natural byproduct of using the Creatrix profile and drivers.

Activating the driving forces of creativity and risk taking is like igniting a source of energy that is already there deep within each of us.

Let's take a closer look at each of the 4As.

Aim

"The greater danger for most of us is not that our aim is too high and we miss it, but that it is too low and we reach it."

Michelangelo

If I say to you, "I want you, your team, or your organization to be more innovative," what does that mean? Without a purpose and a context, the need to innovate loses relevance. Therefore, we begin the innovative process by stating an aim. An aim can be for an individual, a team, or an organization.

The aim may be as simple as wanting to be able to offer more creative ideas in a specific area, such as innovative customer service or alternative ways of delivering a service or program.

Organizations and teams usually need to have clearer aims than individuals do. They need to describe the benefit for trying to achieve greater innovative success. You may have a team that is slowing down, that is, not creating the innovative ideas that it once did, and so they need a boost, a recharge. Or, as with the individual, it may be that the team needs to develop innovative ideas fast to meet the competition head on. Whatever it is, creating an aim is essential for laying the groundwork for increasing innovative capacity.

So what are you aiming for? Are you trying to foster innovation in order to. . .

- Develop new product ideas;
- Create greater efficiencies;
- Reduce the need for working capital;
- Improve customer service;
- Create higher profits; or
- Increase shareholder value?

Aim is all about knowing where you are going. It is not about how you're going to get there. Some people think of aim as the mission or vision. In one sense the aim can be exactly about your mission or vision. If your aim is not congruent with your mission or vision, then some work will need to be done to make them congruent. Additionally, if there is an absence of a clear vision or mission, the importance of this first A, aim, becomes even more pronounced.

There must be a goal or objective. A clear, specific purpose serves as the beginning point from which to frame an opportunity and solution. We all probably know what the aim needs to be with respect to the opportunities facing our organizations. But taking the time to write down these aims brings a clarity that goes beyond our intuitive sense. This can be done alone as the leader of the team or in conjunction with other team members. Examples of aims include the following:

- Increasing our market share;
- Reducing turnover;
- Meeting 80 percent of all salespeople's sales quotas;
- Increasing productivity by 15 percent;
- Going twice as long without an accident this year;
- Ensuring all expense items come in under budget this quarter; or
- Developing six new products in the next six months to address the current market demand.

You get the idea. Each of these aims addresses a specific issue that may require innovative solutions. Table 6.1 provides a set of sample questions that help individuals, teams, and organizations develop their aim. Answers to the questions in the table will help guide you in the right direction toward forming an appropriate aim.

Table 6.1. Questions to Help Develop Aims

Individual Aims

- What areas/ideas are there that you'd like to focus more on? How would they impact your ability to be more effective?
- What are your goals? What do you want to achieve?
- What is your vision for your career five years from now? Ten years from now?
- What's the one single opportunity area that would yield the most results if you focused on it?
- What are your key strengths? Would accentuating these add even greater value to your organization?

Team/Organizational Aims

- How do you work together as a team? What do you see as some of your greatest strengths/weaknesses?
- What do you hope this team/organization can achieve?
- What are some key near-term issues you feel should be addressed?
- Define/describe your organization's vision. Is it being realized? Why or why not?
- How do you see different departments within the organization currently aligning with the vision? How does this impact the organization's effectiveness?
- If you were to describe your team in terms of an image of your future, what would it be? (An image could be a type of car, animal, and so forth—whatever image you might want.) Why did you choose this image?
- What are two or three ideas that you think you need to act on as a team/organization in order to continue to be successful?

Assess

The second A is to assess your current innovative capacity. If you haven't done so already, go back to Chapter 2 and take the Innovation-X Questionnaire and plot yourself on the Creatrix. The assessment process helps you understand whether or not your aim is realistic. You'll use the Creatrix to help with this step. The Creatrix provides insight into your own and your team or organization's current innovative capacity.

As organizations and teams develop their own continuity, they begin to take on signature characteristics. How they view creativity and risk taking will determine how they approach work like problem solving, conflict resolution, and idea generation.

Therefore, it is important to assess the creativity and risk-taking propensities of an organization or team. Knowing whether the organization/team has a high, medium, or low tolerance for creativity and risk taking is important in terms of determining what work needs to be done in order to increase its innovative capacity. To determine a team's profile, simply plot each of the participant's scores on the Creatrix.

The assess step will help you determine if you're aiming too low or too high. For example, if you think you can get a team that profiles as a Modifier to generate ideas like Innovators do, think again. There has to be a real possibility of achieving the aim. If your aim and your profile are too far out of alignment, the team or organization can fail, feel disappointment, and begin blaming others. This backlash is realized all too often when teams take on more than they can handle. Let's use running as a metaphor here to illustrate our point. Wouldn't it be nice to know what distance you're capable of running before signing up for a marathon? Perhaps a half-marathon, ten-miler, or even a ten-kilometer run is more appropriate. Once you know your team's capabilities, you can put a game plan together to make sure they can go the distance.

So how does one determine if an organization, team, or individual is biting off more than they can chew? The process for determining an appropriate aim is rather subjective. In some cases the gap between the current and ideal state is obvious. For example, a new startup company might state that its aim is to develop a new dominant operating platform for the computer industry. In these cases it becomes important to not discourage having such a superordinate goal. Setting a more realistic aim that might allow incremental successes to happen may be a better starting place. For our new computer startup company, this may mean developing software or an operating platform that has distinct competitive advantages for specific markets.

Other times, the aim may be constrained by external forces. These are commonly referred to as barriers to entry. When the barriers to entry are high, there are usually only a few competitors in the market. For example, Coca-Cola and Pepsi-Cola dominate the soft drinks industry. The profitability of these companies indicates room for greater competition, but the barriers to setting up a national distribution network remain substantial. The same principles hold true in the airline industry where the costs of airplanes, gates, hubs, and national advertising costs are prohibitive. In either case, we would encourage organizations in these industries to set aims that are realistic, while still feeding into the superordinate goal. For example, we might suggest becoming the soft drink or airline of choice for a state or region.

In assessing the organization's ability to innovate, it is important to look at its capabilities. Capabilities indicate capacity. Many organizations have the ability to operate at capacity but do not for a variety of reasons. Therefore, the assessment does not put limitations on you or your team. Rather, the assessment helps you to learn exactly what your current capabilities are in order to begin building your innovative capacity.

Activate

Once you understand the organization's, team's, and individuals' orientations, the third A is to activate the creativity and risk-taking drivers. As we've said all along, just knowing that innovation is a function of creativity and risk taking is not enough. Knowing your orientation or your team or organization is great, but what do you do with that information? Activating the seven drivers of creativity and risk taking is how to accelerate innovative capacity.

It's easy to say one needs to be more inner-directed (creativity driver), to become more creative or more resilient (risk-taking driver), or to take more risks. However, the reality is that change is very difficult. Therefore, we recommend focusing only on one or two drivers. Efforts to tackle too many initiatives at once often fail. After you have picked your driver/s, think about what motivated you to select each of these drivers. And think about the stop signs that get in your way.

To activate a driver means to take action in the form of a challenge. Recall the driver quick-check exercise you were asked to complete in Chapter 3. This exercise was designed to help you determine which drivers are important for you to focus on. There is no absolute method for selecting a driver to work on. Some choose to pick the driver they're strongest in and accentuate it, thereby making it a singularly distinctive competency. Others choose a driver that is an obvious stumbling block, thereby providing an area for ample work opportunities. Keep in mind that drivers are interdependent. That is, working on one driver leads to and triggers work on other drivers. It follows then that there is no real right or wrong driver to select. The real work is in challenging yourself in the driver area you selected.

A challenge is designed to help you grow. By challenging yourself, you'll begin developing greater creativity and risk-taking capacity. In Chapter 5 we provided a series of challenges for each of the seven drivers. You can use these to activate work in any one of the drivers, or you can make up your own challenges. Often, people intuitively know which driver to work on, which stop sign is preventing growth, and what specific situations will challenge them most.

The ways in which one challenges oneself can take many forms. Some may challenge themselves to be more disciplined in their risk taking. For example, if authenticity is the selected driver, one might note all of the recent situations in which he or she had the opportunity to be more authentic but failed to do so. Other people working on a creativity driver might choose to make a concerted effort to work more independently. Working more independently can take on a variety of forms in different organizations. In either case, one must first recognize the situations that require driver activation. Only then can one begin working on the driver, a task that, when accomplished, will yield tremendous positive results in terms of personal growth, esteem, and effectiveness that equals innovation.

▶ CASE IN POINT

A team of four HR professionals serves a small Midwestern service company with some sixty-five home office employees and over 1,200 employees in the field nationwide. The aim of the HR team is to become more proactive. Frequently criticized for simply being too reactive, the department head wants to establish the team as one that tackles new initiatives and adds value. The president of the company offers his full support, but much of the executive team remains skeptical. Additional resistance can be found throughout the organization as members historically have been slow to accept changes.

The HR team plots out on the Creatrix as a Modifier team. Together, they elect to focus on the resiliency driver. They know they'll have to become more resilient as they undertake their new initiatives and others express doubt about their ability to change. Cognitive of this, they embark on four new initiatives designed to streamline the HR function. Eliciting help from the executive team as well as general managers in the field is difficult. Frequently met with apathy, Julia, the department head, has to double her resolve to remain resilient as she tries to roll out the new systems. This means recognizing her own stop signs, challenging herself on her ability to be resilient, and developing a "can do" attitude in spite of the resistance and doubting attitudes that she confronts daily.

On completion of the fourth initiative, the HR department celebrates its newfound success. Once a known weak link, the department is held up as a model to the rest of the organization as how to transform oneself into a value-added commodity. All it took was adding a little resiliency. ◀

Apply

"Even if you're on the right track, you'll get run over if you just sit there."

Will Rogers

The fourth A is apply. Apply means to make it happen. You're out of training now; its real time. The aim is clear, the drivers are clear, you've got to incorporate the changes you're making into your everyday functioning. The apply phase is critical. In activating the drivers, the process began. But now, it is up to you to apply the drivers every day in real-life situations with your team and within the organization. This is what actually will help you achieve innovative results.

To apply the driver, approach an opportunity with the driver foremost in your mind. It's precisely this change of perspective in how you approach a problem that leads to greater innovative capacity. Think about what happens when an organization or team together works on the same driver or is at least aware of the others' drivers. There can be continued reinforcement. People can ask one another, "How are you doing?" "Did you give your opinion in the meeting?" "Did you tell that employee no?"

You have to continue applying the drivers until you see noticeable improvement; the length of application time will vary depending on the circumstances, with the goal ultimately being able to create greater innovative responses. Remember, innovative responses needn't be dramatic or large-scale in nature. In fact, innovation does not necessarily mean having to make the next big breakthrough; it can be a simple, cost-effective modification to products, programs, or services. Many innovative responses are rather small. Regardless of scope, the value is in developing the capacity to innovate. *With an increased capacity to innovate, innovations follow.*

We encourage you to create challenges for yourself around the drivers you selected. Experience them in detail from a number of different perspectives. Develop creative ways of reminding yourself about the driver you selected to work on. For example, we write the driver on a colored rubber band that we wear on our wrist to help keep the driver in mind. When an opportunity presents itself and we fail to act, we pull the rubber band to remind us that neglecting the driver is a disservice to our organization and to ourselves. Further, make sure you challenge yourself as it directly relates to your aim. While self-development for its own sake is important, developing innovative capacity as it relates to your aim is critical. Periodically assess how far you've come and what the results have been.

The work that you do around the concepts presented in this chapter will set the tone for your ability to accelerate your innovative capacity. Simply reading the challenges that we talked about in Chapter 5 will do little for your self-development. Taking action to apply the learning from the challenges and translating them into daily actions will yield innovative results. Take the first step by filling in the form in Exhibit 6.1.

Exhibit 6.1. Reaching Your Aims Worksheet

Instructions: Use the following structured worksheet to help you apply your aim.

1. My aim is:

2. The driver I will work on (activate) to reach that aim is:

3. If I were more _____ [insert driver], I would be/do:

4. This stop sign is most likely to get in my way when (give a specific example):

5. These are the two challenges that I will use to activate my driver/s:

6. My daily actions toward greater innovation will include (apply):

▶ CASE IN POINT

A regional manager for a national service organization demands complete, detailed information from all his direct reports before he's willing to make a decision on where or how to reallocate quarterly resources. The problem is that the data for these reports takes up to two weeks to collect from the field units and another week to generate in final report form. By the time the reports reach the regional manager, it's already three weeks into the new quarter. Frequently, the regional manager's analysis takes a week, as he always double-checks everything and makes sure his boss is up-to-speed on the situation. By the time any decisions are made and the resources reallocated, half of the quarter is already gone.

This regional manager's inability to deal with ambiguity causes a number of organizational inefficiencies. The following questions will help surface this manager's issues around creativity and risk taking:

- What might happen if the regional manager were to have a team meeting with his direct reports immediately at the end of each quarter to discuss the situation at length without all of the data?

- What would happen if the regional manager relied on the feedback from his managers versus hard data?

- Are the managers close enough to the business to intuitively know the general trend of the results?

- How could the management team become better able to anticipate business results and thereby reallocate resources in a more timely fashion? ◀

As you can begin to see, the application (apply) portion of the 4As is critical. But it can only occur in succession with the other three A's laying the groundwork. Table 6.2 outlines the 4As of the innovative process.

Table 6.2. The Innovative Process

Aim	Define vision and strategies and articulate your goals for accelerating innovative capacity.
Assess	Take the Innovation-X assessment and then plot individual results on the Creatrix. Use the Creatrix to profile your organization's current capacity to innovate.
Activate	Identify and activate the seven drivers that can help align the organization with the new direction. Practice some of the challenges and understand the stop signs.
Apply	Take action on a daily basis to move to the right on the Innovative Capacity Continuum and to the northeast corner on the Creatrix. Keep your aim in mind and aim toward success!

By now you should have a good understanding of the concepts in the innovative process. It's time to begin translating these into your specific situation. The following examples profile different teams with different group orientations. By illustrating the 4As (aim, assess, activate, and apply) in these examples, we hope to develop your understanding of how to go about building the innovative capacity in your team or organization. After you've had a chance to digest our examples, we invite you to begin sketching out the details of your team or organization.

▶ ORGANIZATION #1: MODEL INC., THE MODIFIER

Background

"Darn it! Another opportunity missed," said Dick, marketing director for Model Inc. "They just weren't thinking out of the box enough. They certainly had the desire to beat their competition, but every time it seemed like the competition was just able to outdo them." It was frustrating because everyone at Model Inc. had a commitment to excellence. They tried so hard to have the best products on the market. However, the customers didn't seem to care so much that their products were the highest quality; they seemed to want more functions, bells, and whistles. The time to make some dramatic changes was now.

Aim

The leadership team met every Thursday afternoon. They had been doing this for years. Today was no exception. What was an exception was today's speaker, who talked about the future of the industry. She spoke about new technologies and customer expectations. It was the vice president for HR who had the idea for bringing her in. Surprisingly, the speaker knew a lot about Model Inc.'s competition. Not only did the competition have great customer service systems, but they also had great R&D and marketing departments that were staying on top of customer expectations all the time. Model Inc. had severely cut back its R&D department five years ago when times were tough.

The leadership team was in denial. Most thought that the competition was too radical in product design. However, the truth was that modifying their existing products wasn't going to cut it. They needed new product ideas to serve increasingly diverse market niches to survive. Their aim had to be to focus more on the needs of the customer. By the end of the meeting, it was clear to them that there were some serious issues that had to be addressed immediately.

Assess

The Creatrix profile of the organization (see Figure 6.2) showed why they were in this predicament; members were almost all Modifiers with a few Sustainers, a couple of Planners, one Innovator, and a Dreamer. No one really paid any attention to the Innovator; he was viewed as too impetuous.

Figure 6.2. Creatrix for Model Inc.

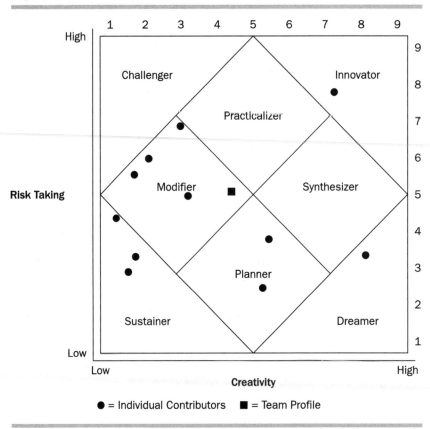

When they first saw their profile, they realized how important it was for them to start using the Innovator and Dreamer that they had. People recognized that they'd come up with some pretty interesting ideas, but they were always dismissed as being too weird. Now they seemed pretty creative. In fact, some of the same ideas had been implemented by the competition, albeit with slight variations. The board chair stated that the time had come to change their Modifier profile to meet the increasing pressures from stiff competition.

Activate

Model Inc.'s drivers showed that members' ability to accept others working independently was virtually nonexistent. They seemed to micromanage everything. People had little trust that others would do a good job. Further, their preference for fixed systems over ambiguity was coming through loud and clear. They rarely allowed an idea to percolate and seemed to manage the risk out of everything.

In order to develop greater innovative capacity, they selected independence and ambiguity as the drivers to work on. Each team member worked on the driver from an individual as well as a team perspective. Every time an example of their inability to deal with ambiguity or lack of independence reared its ugly head, they challenged one another to show more acceptance of the unknown and to let people have more opportunity to add their own thoughts to the discussion.

This process seemed excruciatingly painful and chaotic at times, but it was exactly what the organization needed. Working more independently and tolerating greater levels of ambiguity were certainly significant challenges, but these were not insurmountable. By challenging themselves in these areas, they greatly increased their odds of success by becoming more risk tolerant and creative.

Apply

Model Inc. made a conscious choice to start bringing in people with greater creative and risk-taking orientations—Innovators, Synthesizers, and Dreamers. And by working more independently and allowing for greater ambiguity, they began to build their innovative capacity. At first this caused more failures than successes, but it seemed like a fair tradeoff, given the gravity of their situation. Within a short time, they were able to see the benefits of applying these drivers. It took them down paths they never imagined before, which made many people uncomfortable, but at the same time produced unconventional solutions to their daunting business challenges. ◀

▶ ORGANIZATION #2: PLANET PARTNERS, LLC, THE PLANNER

Background

PLANet had a well-laid-out process for going global. It was a terrific strategic plan designed to integrate its newly acquired businesses in Europe and Asia. Everyone was confident and proud when it was unveiled. It called for initial growth through acquisition and then by a comprehensive marketing plan, first in Europe, followed by Asia. Managers from the United States were put in charge. The company hand-selected these managers because they exhibited strong corporate values and knew how the other companies within the United States operated. Two new European companies had recently been added to PLANet Corporation. Initially, their bottom line was excellent and everything seemed to indicate they were in line for another great year.

Despite this promising beginning, something unusual began to happen. First, revenues began to slip, followed by a downturn in profitability. Costs began creeping up, and employee turnover began to rise. It soon became apparent that things were not going according to plan. What had worked in the United States was not translating well to European and Asian counterparts. However, no one really wanted to address the issues. The marginal results were tolerated until it came time to implement shared services. New challenges arose requiring innovative solutions. But any time a new idea was proposed, it didn't seem to fit the plan. The company was in trouble.

Aim

Initially the plan worked well. But with the new challenges from Europe and Asia, the plan seemed ill-suited for sustaining growth. The problems extended beyond cultural integration. Not only were the sales and marketing approaches different, but the ways problems were seen and potentially resolved were also different. Eventually, the company decided that it needed to abandon the plan. PLANet's aim was to determine how to decentralize operations to maximize results while still maintaining governance.

Assess

PLANet's assessment results profiled the executive leadership of the organization as largely Planners (see Figure 6.3). Consequently, the organization was low in both creativity and risk taking. It also had a large number of Sustainers and Modifiers.

Figure 6.3. Creatrix for PLANet

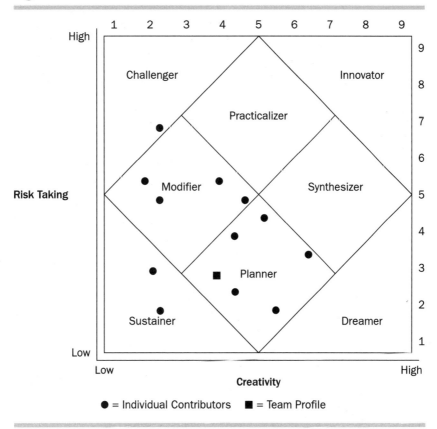

● = Individual Contributors   ■ = Team Profile

This meant that the things they did, they did very well. They kept the business going, but kept it going in the same ways as they always had. What had made them successful in the past had become a potential liability.

Activate

The creativity driver of accepting uniqueness was very low. Members of PLANet's leadership team did not seem to recognize and value the uniqueness of their global business partners. Rather than embracing the diversity of their counterparts throughout the world, they tried to convert all operations to U.S. business styles.

Their risk-taking drivers indicated a relatively low level of authenticity and moderate levels of resiliency and self-acceptance. The low level of authenticity stemmed from a somewhat half-hearted attempt to recognize global diversity, thus causing an overly political approach to simple cultural differences.

As a group, they decided to tackle the drivers of uniqueness and authenticity. This meant recognizing the uniqueness of their European and Asian counterparts. Moreover, it meant using the unique skills their world-wide counterparts brought to the organization.

Apply

This was a scary time for PLANet. The company had never abandoned a plan before. They knew they needed to change their Creatrix profile either by challenging themselves on their own drivers or by adding complementary personnel. The task of changing their organizational profile was too daunting. They put together a new leadership team of Innovators, Synthesizers, and Practicalizers from representatives throughout the world. This European-led team was able to make enough swift adjustments to save PLANet from further self-destruction. ◄

► ORGANIZATION #3: ITEC.COM, THE INNOVATOR

Background

Company ITEC.com is in chaos. Although it has designed some of the most innovative systems for tracking clients and products that can be found anywhere, it has no compatible systems; virtually nothing is fully integrated. The personnel assigned to make sure that the systems are up and running every day are completely reactive.

ITEC.com was incorporated two years ago. Revenues and returns are dismal. Stockholders are beginning to question the viability of the operation. The CEO knows there's a problem. In fact, he knows there are many problems. But rather than direct his energies toward systemic problem solving, he directs all of his energies toward anticipating future trends.

When the CEO calls meetings, he is never really sure what kind of turnout he will get. Everyone seems to be too busy. It's not a lack of expertise, money, or even product demand that ails this organization.

Aim

ITEC.com's CEO has just read *The Innovation Equation* on a return flight from an out-of-town board of directors meeting. He calls a staff meeting and about three-fourths of the employees show up. They're waiting to hear what the next big idea is that they're going to work on. Everyone knows that the last big idea, like the one before, only lasted for a short time. Yet everyone is continually being reminded that this is a fast-paced, dynamic, technology-driven industry that has to be responsive to the marketplace. However, the CEO begins by stating that the company is in trouble. He confesses that the financial results have been poor, further stating that if the company is to remain viable, it is going to require permanent solutions to some of its most pressing problems.

Acknowledging that this company was founded on innovative thinking, he reminds employees that revenue generation and profitability sustain businesses. The objective is to bring each project through to fruition before taking on new initiatives.

Assess

ITEC.com is fairly small. It has fewer than seventy-five employees and yet has some of the brightest people in the computer industry on staff. Company leadership knows that it has to be clear about what's getting in its way. Yet no one seems to be able to pull it all together. The fact is they probably don't have anyone on board who knows how to pull it all together.

When ITEC.com assembled its Creatrix profile, it became clear what the problem was (see Figure 6.4). Virtually the entire senior management team's profile was high in both creativity and risk taking. Almost everyone was an Innovator.

Figure 6.4. Creatrix for ITEC.com

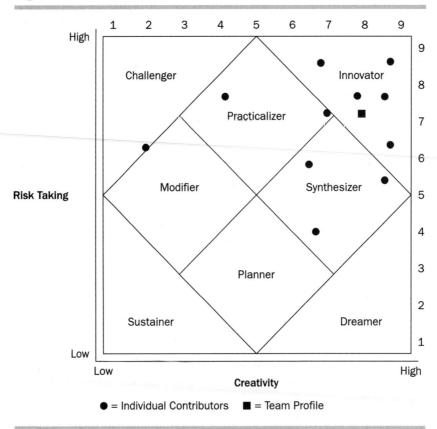

Employees always seemed to have many good ideas, but there was rel-atively little follow-through on any of their projects. What this group needed was to rein in on the multiple strategic initiatives rather than build greater capacity.

Activate

ITEC.com's team profiled very high on all of the drivers. Rather then need-ing to focus in on what drives creativity and risk taking, they needed to do just the opposite. Pushing harder on any one of the drivers wouldn't yield better results. In fact, it would only serve to exacerbate the existing conditions. Therefore, rather than activating the drivers, they need to implement a different strategy.

Apply

In order to move this organization forward, ITEC.com needs to find more Planners, Modifiers, and Sustainers to help implement the ideas. A focus on a systems discipline approach to project management will help. These are the invaluable skill sets that the Planners, Modifiers, and Sustainers bring to the organization. A Practicalizer may help bridge the gap between the ideas of the Innovators and the skills of the implementers. These people can immediately recognize whether or not an idea can happen and will help cull from the many ideas present.

With this application of the Creatrix, the systems integration will improve and project implementation will be aided. The idea here is not to lose the Innovators, but rather to add to the profile with complementary skill sets, thereby making it possible for the organization to strategically grow by establishing solid project management plans rather than jumping from idea to idea without closure. ◀

Takeaways from the Stories

- Every organization needs a balance of all the orientations.
- Be conscious of the times when you need more of one orientation than another.
- Building the capacity for greater innovation requires activating the drivers necessary to move toward the upper right-hand quadrant of the Creatrix.
- Build your teams for what you need. If you need creative and breakthrough kinds of ideas, put your Innovators and Synthesizers on that team. If you need only slight changes to an idea, put your Modifiers, Planners, and Practicalizers together. If you need no changes, then call on your Sustainers. If you need someone to stir things up and get you off the dime, use your Challengers; and if you seem to have exhausted every alternative, call on a Dreamer.
- Don't accept the current Creatrix profile as the only reality. You may need a different mix of orientations in the future. Create it.

Use the following form to profile your own team or organization.

▶ ORGANIZATION #4: YOUR TEAM/ORGANIZATION

Background

Aim

Assess

Activate

Apply

◀

The 4As—aim, assess, activate, and apply—should be intuitively appealing. It simply means figuring out where your team needs or wants to go, determining your ability to get there, shoring up your weaknesses and accentuating your strengths, and applying your skills and newfound knowledge to the problem or obstacle.

In the concluding chapters we talk about the innovative leader and consultant. Whether you're developing yourself or assisting another in becoming a better leader, the concepts we discuss in Chapter 7 will help you get there. In Chapter 8, our discussion about creativity and risk taking as precepts for the effective practitioner is important to the development of the individual consultant's innovative capacity.

Ideas for the Consultant

If working with teams or setting the stage for working with an entire organization:

- Explain the 4As and why the framework is useful.

- Ask people to share the stories of their own organizations. Contrast them with the stories in this chapter. In what ways are the stories similar?

- Have individuals create a personal aim. Provide some examples, a patent they've had in mind, a recipe, a song, or poem they've been working on.

- Have the organization or team create an aim together. Have them brainstorm all kinds of aims for which they'd like to see innovative ideas developed.

- Link the aim they've developed with the driver and stop sign they've identified.

  Here's the aim that I/we need to focus on:

  Here's the driver that will help me/us get there:

  Here's the stop sign that could get in our way:

- Use a methodology, such as brainstorming, role plays, or the Creatrix "Ba" (Appendix B) to develop new ideas.

7

The Innovative Leader

"What man dare, I dare."

William Shakespeare, Macbeth

TO BE AN INNOVATIVE LEADER, you must do four things well:

1. Create an innovative culture;

2. Set an innovative aim;

3. Become more innovative yourself; and

4. Create innovative teams.

In this chapter we examine each of these four key attributes of innovative leaders.

Create an Innovative Culture

[The leader's] "own competence depends upon a deeper self-knowledge
and a clear understanding of others if he is to gain their cooperation
and to succeed in fusing business practices with human motivation."

Alfred Marrow

According to the classic book on culture, *Corporate Cultures: The Rites and Rituals of Corporate Life,* authored by Terence E. Deal and Allen A. Kennedy (1982), the building blocks of culture include the rites and rituals of an organization and its values, management and communication styles, structure, business environment, and heroes. It is therefore no wonder that we can make the statement that culture defines the organization.

All teams and organizations have identifiable cultures. These cultures are complex in nature and are a function of many variables. Culture significantly influences how an organization operates. Strong cultures bring people together around a common set of principles, values, and an operating style that enables them to feel part of something bigger than themselves. Strong cultures enable organizations to succeed. Yet, because of its equivocal nature, culture is dismissed in this scientific and rational world of ours. But examine why it is that most acquisitions, mergers, and even internal change efforts fail within an organization, and you'll find that most often it's because the issue of culture was not given sufficient weight in the process.

Consider for a moment the rites and rituals of organizations. For organizations that tend to have a process type of culture, many meetings are held in order to come to resolution on an action or decision. In this type of culture, it may take months to make a decision. But when it is made, everyone has had a say in the outcome. Consider other organizations where the rites and rituals around decision making are different, perhaps one where *you* are empowered to make decisions—where the edict is full speed ahead and we'll deal with the consequences, if any, later.

In more formal organizations, communication patterns tend to take the form of written correspondence with copies to everyone. Actions are not taken without the appropriate documentation. In less formal organizations, people will walk down the hall and talk about what needs to happen, and it does.

In some companies, successes are recognized with great hoopla. Rewards are given and people participate in events designed primarily for visibility. In other companies, the success is quietly acknowledged by a thank you and everyone goes back to business as usual.

No one culture is right or wrong. Each culture more than likely has some very positive attributes as well as some undesirable characteristics. Creating the perfect culture is not an appropriate goal; creating a culture that fosters the types of behaviors that make your organization successful and desirable is. If you are trying to make a change in the rites and rituals and communication patterns within an organization, one thing is certain: You need to first understand its culture.

In terms of creativity and risk taking, some cultures foster and encourage creativity and risk taking through written principles and statements. Others incorporate them into their unwritten rules and model them through their practices. Table 7.1 contains a series of organizational messages that can inhibit creativity, risk taking, and innovation.

Table 7.1. Organizational Messages That Inhibit Innovation

- The bottom line is the name of the game.

- Wall Street determines how you make decisions or, for government entities, taxpayers are the driving force.

- Know the outcome of a project or initiative in advance of its undertaking. The organization craves predictability at all costs.

- Failure punished with messages like: "Don't try that again."

- Mistakes swept under the carpet because the organization doesn't want people to think that mistakes are acceptable.

- Cash cows valued over everything else because predictability is considered essential to success.

- Conflict frowned on because it indicates you are not a team player.

- Conformity desired because it indicates you are a team player.

It doesn't take long for a new member of the team or organization to know what kind of culture they've just become part of. One usually gains a fair sense of the organization's culture immediately by observing the interactions of team members. Think for a moment about an organization you belong to and how willing or unwilling it is to accept new ideas (creativity) and drive change to implement new ideas (risk taking). Consider this fictitious exchange overheard at the water cooler:

Person A   "I think we should try [insert any idea or issue]."
Person B   "We tried that several years ago. It didn't work."

What does this simple exchange reflect about the way ideas are valued in the organization? What are the bigger messages being sent to Person A? Just because something didn't work once before doesn't mean it won't work in the future. Things, people, and attitudes change. Many ideas fail for reasons other than the idea itself. A good idea will surely falter if key members don't support its implementation or the right resources aren't put behind it.

Breakthrough thinking begins with breaking down the barriers that stifle creativity and risk taking. The rules around creativity and risk taking in an organization are usually unwritten. Consequently, we find out what the rules are by bumping into them, rather than being told what they are in advance. Imagine what might happen in your organization if you provided a roadmap for learning about innovation, rather than languishing in an environment where the status quo is sacred and protected.

To set an innovative culture, you must move from the comfort and security of always reducing risk to welcoming and embracing the uncertainty of risk. This means developing authenticity, becoming more resilient, and learning to be more self-accepting. Just as culture obliges behavior, behavior recurs only with nurturing. This is the classic question: "Which came first, the chicken or the egg?" By the very nature of these characteristics, we know that this means the organization that takes more risks will make more mistakes. The hockey great Wayne Gretzky once said, "You miss 100 percent of the shots you don't take."

Remember, we don't advocate risk for risk's sake. Nor do we suggest taking unbridled risks. However, appropriate risks are healthy for the organization. Everything you try won't work. Accept it. We're human, we make mistakes, and we fail. The key is to learn from our mistakes. Don't fear the iterative process.

Similarly, you'll need to foster creativity in your culture by tolerating more ambiguity, by encouraging independence and inner-directedness in both yourself and your team members, and by learning to embrace uniqueness.

Our research indicates that a person's creativity diminishes with the length of time he or she spends in one organization. This is a function of becoming steeped in the history and culture of an organization. Concerted efforts must be made to overcome these tendencies.

Developing an innovative culture is hard work. It means changing paradigms. It means doing things differently from the past. Change creates chaos. Using the drivers in this process helps you change your culture in a way that fosters growth rather than creates anxiety.

Keep in mind that to create an innovate culture you need to lead with the drivers of creativity and risk taking. How that is manifested in each team or organization will be unique to the application of the drivers. That is, each of the seven drivers as manifested individually and collectively as a team is not prescriptive in nature or replicable. To try and capture it as such would only drive out the very thing we're advocating: creativity and risk taking.

Set an Innovative Aim

"Aim for the highest."

Andrew Carnegie

The innovative leader helps to set the direction for the organization or, in our words, the aim. What do you hope to gain for yourself and the entire organization by building innovation? Be specific in your aim. Is the focus on servicing customers (internal and external) in new ways, finding new advantages over competitors, or exploiting company strengths?

An innovative aim means setting a direction that incites action in team members. An aim that doesn't do this isn't really innovative; it's just an aim. For example, if I state my aim as "to increase our market share by 5 percent," I have satisfied the requirement of stating a clear goal. However, think about what this might mean to different people in the organization. Albeit a worthy goal, under your direction, it might simply mean we stay the course and work harder! Not exactly the kind of leadership that will leave a legacy.

Let's look at the same aim in innovative terms. The superordinate goal is to increase market share by 5 percent. If we think in innovative terms, we need to ask ourselves what leads to increased market share. In this case, it might be a function of advertising, sales, product innovations, and customer service. Each person on the team will need to approach the commission to increase market share in terms that he or she understands.

Perhaps an appropriate innovative aim in this case is to have each department head identify one or two actionable items that will lead to increasing overall sales. If the customer service manager pushes back and says, "Hey, that's the sales department's job," well, then you know you're moving toward the right innovative aim. Increasing market share is everyone's job! And if the customer service manager doesn't see how his department contributes to the overall success of the company in terms of increasing market share, then it's time for a long talk.

Innovative aims push people out of their comfort zones. They challenge people to think, take risks, and become creative. A truly remarkable change will begin as you learn to shift your thinking from the routine and normal to encouraging risks and creativity in your people and yourself.

Become More Innovative Yourself

"Nothing is truly yours until you understand it—not even yourself."
Warren Bennis, On Becoming a Leader

Many organizational leaders are unaware of how much they impact their organizational culture. Often they profess to want greater creativity and risk taking, yet their own actions are contradictory. For example, many leaders profess to want an authentic culture, one that enables people to be themselves and talk openly about the tough issues. Yet they all too frequently rule with a heavy hand, coming down so hard on diverse opinions that they don't even realize that their very own actions speak louder than their words, thereby creating the political environment they espouse to dislike so much.

You must continually work to increase your own innovative capacities if you want others to increase theirs. Challenging yourself on your selected drivers does this. Additionally, you must be a champion of innovation in others. Encouraging and rewarding creativity and risk taking, as evidenced in the drivers, does this. If you're not doing this yourself and are requiring it in others, your teams will not develop their innovative capacity. The innovative leader practices what he or she preaches. Without creativity, how can you create an innovative aim? And how can you generate creative ideas and have others take risks if you're not willing to take the risk to make it happen? Leaders who understand themselves are those who have the greatest impact on others. All the leader's words and actions, including his or her values and beliefs about creativity and risk taking, are what people are paying attention to. Remember, one's attitudes are highly visible.

To begin the process of understanding your own innovative capacity is to start by understanding your own creative and risk-raking orientation. Are you a Planner, Modifier, Practicalizer, Synthesizer, Innovator, Dreamer, Sustainer, or Challenger? Table 7.2 provides some insight into the orientations as they impact your leadership style.

Table 7.2. Orientation Insights for the Innovative Leader

Creatrix Orientation	As a Leader	Self-Understanding (What Others Think/See)
Planner	You operate with a need for order and plans. Creative ideas fit within the plans. You are going to need more information and data before taking a risk. You may appear to others as too data-driven—not using your "instincts" as a leader.	People will check with you for clarity. You also may be checking in too often to determine whether others are in sync with the plan. Some of the most valuable contributions may occur outside the plan.
Modifier	You believe in incremental changes and tweaking existing ideas. You are not going to take risks unless you can see the real benefits.	You'll be the first asked if a new product/service without a lot of newfangled stuff is needed. However, you may appear to others as not seeing the bigger picture.
Practicalizer	You're willing to try something as long as it is practical. You don't want a lot of "harebrained" ideas coming at you all at once. You keep the targeted aim in front of you at all times.	Moving creative ideas through the organization will be seen as your specialty. However, you may be so focused on the practical application of an idea that you miss an important breakthrough opportunity.

Table 7.2. Orientation Insights for the Innovative Leader, Cont'd

Creatrix Orientation	As a Leader	Self-Understanding (What Others Think/See)
Synthesizer	You see possibilities in everything and put unlikely combinations of things together to create something new. You are willing to take risks, but not at all costs. You are a cautious risk taker.	You will develop some of the most unique ideas and will amaze people with what you put together. However, people may have a hard time initially tracking with you; so you may lose them unless they can see how you moved from point A to point B.
Innovator	You have a new idea every minute and may drive people within the organization crazy trying to keep up with you. While you are trying to keep ahead of the curve, they're trying to keep up with you, and you can wear them out.	You provide much value in keeping an organization on the cutting edge. However, your multitude of ideas without complete follow-through may appear too chaotic for some.
Dreamer	You come up with lots of great ideas but often don't share them or know how to drive them forward. People may look for direction from you as to how to "make it happen," but you may not be able to take it to that level.	People like your ideas, but you have difficulty implementing them. Your low propensity for risk taking inhibits your innovative capacity.
Sustainer	You like stability and prefer to maintain the status quo. You provide a lot of stability for an organization. However, when people come to you with new ideas, you appear resistant.	Your stability brings strength to an organization that wants to change focus frequently. However, you may appear resistant to any change and any new ideas.
Challenger	You have the attitude of let's keep moving. You are ready to take action. You can drive ideas forward, but they usually are not your own ideas. However, because you don't let much get by you, you may appear critical to others.	You're always on the ball ready to respond. However, you may appear abrasive and insensitive. As a result, people may become resistant to sharing their creative ideas with you.

The innovative leader is on a journey to self-improvement. Innovative leaders seek challenges to calibrate their abilities. They seek to understand themselves in order to understand the impact they have on others. If they want to further understand their creative and risk-taking abilities, innovative leaders must look to the seven drivers and understand how their personal drivers affect their capacity to become more creative and take more risks. Recall the need to activate the drivers. Select a driver to work on and focus on understanding it and utilizing it to drive greater innovation within yourself and your organization.

Create Innovative Teams

"When the best leader's work is done, the people will say,
'We did it ourselves.'"

Lao-Tzu

While there is no one formula for creating a dream team, there are a few key principles to help guide the process. Keep in mind that we're talking about building a dream team with respect to creating greater innovative capacity, specifically driving creativity and risk taking. We are not talking about matching appropriate skill sets to tasks or providing training.

Creating an innovative team is a function of developing an innovative culture, setting an innovative aim, and becoming more innovative yourself. Do these things first before moving on to constructing an innovative team for the greatest success. The innovative leader knows that he or she cannot have an entire team or organization filled with Innovators because that will mean chaos; nor can one have teams filled only with Sustainers because nothing will ever change. The innovative leader knows how to construct different types of teams for different types of successes.

Creating innovative teams begins with making sure you understand the value of each Creatrix orientation. With a thorough understanding of the orientations, you'll be able to build a team that reflects the appropriate levels of creativity and risk taking. For example, Modifier or Planner teams will benefit from adding a Synthesizer, Practicalizer, or Innovator. Innovative teams will benefit by adding Sustainers and Planners. And Synthesizer and Dreamer teams will benefit by adding a Challenger or Practicalizer.

With an innovative culture, an innovative aim, a commitment to becoming more innovative yourself, and a team with an appropriate orientation profile, you'll be poised to meet your organizational challenges with greater innovative efforts. The final piece is to keep the drivers topmost, that is, figure out ways to incorporate the drivers in all of your organization's activities. For example, placing signs or posters naming the drivers in hallways and meeting rooms helps generate constant awareness. Further, it provides a forum for challenging someone on one of the drivers. Another technique is to schedule regular reviews of team activities using the Innovative Capacity Continuum. It really doesn't matter what techniques are used to keep the driver topmost; what's important is the constant, rigorous follow-up to acting on the drivers.

► CASE IN POINT

The Fall Management Conference for InOvate Company

It is July, the time of year that InOvate Company always begins its planning process for the fall management conference. Managers across the multinational company have already been given notice that they have to block their calendars from October 15th through the 17th. There may be some adjustments in that time frame, but everyone has been asked to hold it for the next month at least.

InOvate is a manufacturing company that has grown from a $500 million to a $1.5 billion company in less than five years. The leadership has high hopes for continuing this level of growth. They'd like to double their size in the next three years.

The new CEO is expected to impart his vision for the company in advance of the management conference, laying out the "big picture." The word is out that his vision for the company is moving from a highly decentralized organization to a much more centralized one. Everyone is concerned because this is a big change of direction. The questions are already being asked—how can we possibly do this? Statements like "This isn't our culture" and "We are going to be giving up our autonomy" are heard everywhere. There are also some stirrings about the possibility of more acquisitions, even though the recent mergers are still unsettled.

The CEO is concerned about the meeting. This is his first management conference as CEO; he had been COO for the last five years. He wants the conference to be successful. In an effort to make it successful, he has asked for the advice and participation of key staff members. The only directive he gives them is that he does not want it to be the same old stuff; he wants something new and refreshing—he wants to leave his mark on the organization as the new CEO. He wants the conference to be innovative because that's what he wants from the entire company over the next three years. This conference will set the stage for the new direction.

The new planning team for the conference just received a message from the chair of the planning team with the following list of questions to consider:

- What kinds of topics should be addressed at the conference?
- How should they be considered?
- What should the outcomes be?
- How should it be rolled out?
- Who should be involved?
- Are there things that should happen prior to the conference— pre-planning ideas?

The CEO has selected people he thinks will provide a wide perspective. When the staff he asked to advise meets to discuss the conference, they agree to divide into two teams. One team will conceptualize the bigger picture and develop creative ideas that will help make the conference truly different; the other team will be responsible for carrying out the idea and implementing it, although they too have the opportunity to add some creative ways of implementing the program.

Here is how the teams are divided. The first team includes:

- Chuck the Challenger,
- Sheila the Synthesizer,
- Dan the Dreamer, and
- Peter the Practicalizer.

Team one includes mostly the orientations that are going to feel comfortable with developing ideas that haven't been thought of before. The Practicalizer will provide some concreteness for the ideas that the Synthesizer and the Dreamer will create. The Challenger will also make sure that they stay on track and, together with the Practicalizer, will help to drive the ideas forward.

The second team includes:

· Mike the Modifier,

· Sally the Sustainer,

· Ian the Innovator, and

· Pat the Planner.

Team two includes the orientations that are going to plan the conference from beginning to end in a deliberate fashion. It includes the Planner, who has an eye for charting a thorough course, and a Sustainer, who'll know how to capture all of the details. The Modifier will be sure to tweak some of the ideas that have come from team one to make it just right. However, with the Innovator on this team, there is the risk of chaos, but he or she will add new ideas that could make the implementation part of the program pretty exciting. You might add a Practicalizer to this team, as he or she will ferret out the ideas that may be a little too innovative. Would you include someone else on either team? What orientation would the person have? ◀

Are you beginning to see how creating the right team for the right tasks can make a powerful difference? The innovative leader understands not only his or her own impact, but also how to leverage the different orientations to obtain the best results. The innovative leader knows what each orientation contributes and the hindrances and contributions of his or her orientation. This leader also knows what it means in terms of his or her position and effectiveness as a leader. You can use the worksheet in Exhibit 7.1 to help plan your teams.

After the work is completed, step back and ask yourself, "How did the team do?" Did they in fact get the job done? Now ask whether you are prepared:

• To create an innovative culture;

• To set an innovative aim;

• To become innovative yourself; and

• To create innovative teams.

Then do it!

In the next chapter we discuss practical aspects for the innovative practitioner.

Exhibit 7.1. Worksheet to Create an Innovative Team

Exercise: State your aim and put a team together that will do the best job of reaching your aim.

Aim:

_____

What orientations are needed?   Who on your team has this orientation?

Orientations Needed	Team Members with This Orientation

Ideas for the Consultant

When working with an individual leader in a coaching situation:

- Review the four components of an innovative leader.

- Discuss the concepts of creativity, risk taking, and innovation in detail.

- Have participants take the assessment and understand their own drivers and stop signs. Discuss strategies for building innovative capacity.

- Have participants reflect on the aims they have for their organization/team. With their newfound understanding of themselves, have them think about and discuss the kinds of innovations that have been created within the team/organization and what they might do to foster innovation within the organization both in terms of their own orientation and in the team/organization as a whole.

8

The Innovative Consultant

"If we listened to our intellect, we'd never have a love affair. We'd never have a friendship. We'd never go into business, because we'd be cynical. Well, that's nonsense. You've got to jump off cliffs all the time and build your wings on the way down."

Ray Bradbury

TO HAVE AN IMPACT on today's organizations, OD consultants must be focused on increasing their own innovative capacity. You need to model the behaviors you expect in others if you want them to follow your lead.

To be effective OD consultants, we are required to lead rather than follow; create rather than replicate; expand rather than contract. We must continually learn, develop, and renew ourselves in order to serve the dynamic organizations seeking our assistance. The self-development and renewal process is unique to every one of us. However, two basic elements remain constant, regardless of the size or scope of your practice: The need to be creative and the ability to take risks. These basic elements are the very heart of being an effective OD practitioner. Our success will be short-lived unless we're able to develop our own creativity and risk taking in the work that we do with individuals, teams, and organizations.

As OD practitioners, we are required to practice the competencies we teach others. But without these two OD leadership basics, *creativity* and *risk taking*, it would not be possible for us to succeed. For example, without creativity, how can you create a vision with your clients? And how can you make a vision happen if you're not willing to take risks? A vision without risk taking never happens.

As consultants, creativity means looking outside your immediate purview—being on alert for new ideas coming down the pike and looking for creative new trends that may impact you and your client organizations. The successful OD consultant knows that creative solutions exist; we just have to find them.

> "If you are seeking creative ideas, go out walking. Angels whisper to a man when he goes for a walk."
>
> *Raymond Inmon*

To be an effective OD consultant also means taking the risk to "walk your talk." It's easy to walk and talk your values when you're not faced with a challenge. But if your values run against the norm, then there's a risk. How much easier is it just to go along with a client than stand your ground? How difficult is it to take the risk to walk your values—to risk losing a client?

Stop for a moment and ask yourself the questions: "Would I have been a stronger consultant had I been willing to take more risks with that client? Could I have made more of a difference if I had been willing to use my own capacity for creativity and risk taking?" Surely, all of us will answer this question in the affirmative because we've all had opportunities to be more creative and take more risks than we have chosen to take.

As an OD consultant, what does it mean to be creative and to take risks? Understanding your own creativity and risk-taking propensities is essential for leveraging these two elements in client systems. Table 8.1 provides a list of creativity and risk-taking considerations for consultants.

Table 8.1. Creativity and Risk-Taking Attributes for Consultants

Creativity for OD Consultants	Risk Taking for OD Consultants
Modify an existing intervention, game, or simulation	Take on a program/project never done before
Use new ways to understand the culture and the client	Collaborate with colleagues
	State your limitations or areas of expertise
Take on new clients	Trust the process
Modify existing tools to enhance or leverage learning	Call an individual/team on inappropriate behaviors
Create a dynamite new intervention, game, or simulation	Name tough issues
	Tell a client that he or she is off-base
Incorporate nontraditional methodologies (for example, storytelling, analogical mediated inquiry) into your practice	Work with new clients
	Use a new tool, simulation, or exercise
Create probing questions that get at the heart of the issue	Address a conflict
	Confess to not having all the answers

Understanding that you need to be creative and take risks is not enough. That's akin to realizing you need more education but not enrolling in a class or starting a self-study program. Rather than wonder how to become more creative or to take more risks, we asked ourselves, "What drives creativity and risk taking?"

By now we certainly know that it is the seven drivers of creativity and risk taking. To use these drivers effectively, we must find the right balance within both our client systems and ourselves. The more we learn and understand these drivers, the more we increase our ability to be creative and take more risks. These are basic elements of our jobs as OD practitioners.

The drivers shown in Figure 8.1 illustrate the relationship between the drivers (far left) for creativity and risk taking and the OD consultant. The drivers provide concrete ways of moving forward; they give us a handle on what we need to work on in order to become more creative and take more risks—concepts that enable action with individuals, teams, and organizations.

Figure 8.1. The Drivers' Relationship to the OD Consultant

To apply the drivers, you must develop an appreciation for how they influence behavior. For example, ambiguity can be viewed as either threatening or liberating. Do you walk into an intervention with everything planned? If the plan isn't followed, do you feel as though you've failed? The ability to appreciate ambiguity and accept it as a given enables you to develop the right processes for the client. It allows you to change in midstream and to accept change.

So too with resiliency. Being able to rebound from rejection is a learned behavior that enables us to take more risks and recover more quickly from our mistakes. Making mistakes or being rejected as practitioners is inevitable. How we react to these learning opportunities is critical. Learning how to become more resilient helps us to persevere in a challenging business climate or when dealing with a challenging client.

The Drivers in Action for an OD Consultant

Here are some examples from our work with clients from which you can see the creativity and risk-taking drivers in action. The first example shows how one consultant had to be both creative and willing to take a risk.

▶ THE COACHING PROGRAM

After working for the same client for eight years, it had become a challenge to remain creative and take risks. Jean loved the work she did with the client and depended on the income stream. The client also depended on

Jean to continually be creative and take risks to help them be the kind of organization they strove to be.

Recently, Jean had the challenge of designing an executive coaching program for them. She struggled to find fresh material, as she had used virtually every exercise she could think of with the client before. She was challenged to provide something that would send one message home: Be positive when coaching young executives.

Here's what she came up with: playing checkers. She divided the soon-to-be coaches into three groups. Each team set out a checkerboard while the coaches assigned to each of the players met with Jean. There was a nervous tension in the room. The leadership team looked at Jean as if she were crazy. After all, having a group of senior executives play checkers may not seem appropriate. She could have folded at that point and said, "OK, if you don't want to play, we won't." But she didn't; she talked about why they didn't want to play. They thought it was just a game, with no real value. She explained the value would become clearer as the exercise unfolded. They reluctantly agreed by accepting the ambiguity of the situation at hand and so did Jean; she hadn't used this exercise before. She trusted her own skills and her own capacity to bounce back and be resilient if it didn't work.

The coaches were given the following instructions: "Sit behind your player and whisper negative messages as the game is being played, such as, 'Well, you could have done that better,' 'You could have thought about that move a little longer before you took that step,' *or* 'Why did you make that move; didn't you see what she was going to do?'" In the second round, they switched whom they were coaching and were told to whisper only positive messages, such as, "Great move; how did you think of that?" *or* "Wow—nice job, *and* keep up the good work!"

In debriefing the exercise, Jean encouraged people to think about what was helpful and not helpful in each coaching experience. As a result, it crystallized the power of positive messages and the impact of negative messages on coachees. In the end, everyone said they were glad that they'd continued with the checkers, even though it initially made them uncomfortable. Together, both the consultant and client showed a willingness to accept ambiguity and take a risk. ◀

In the second example, Dirk needs to be authentic with his client. By being authentic, he is able to both realize the importance of authenticity and model it for the client.

▶ TEAM BUILDING . . . SHHH!

Recently a client came to Dirk. He had worked with her many times when she held another position within the organization. So it was really out of character when she asked him whether he could do team building, but not call it that. "Tell me more," Dirk replied without immediately indicating his uneasiness about her indirectness. She said, "They don't like words like team building." "So what are we doing this for?" Dirk asked. "Well, no one really talks to each other. They go behind each other's backs and talk about what's not working. They're not supportive of the overall organizational issues; they only care about their own groups." She concluded, "They need team building, but they just don't know it."

Dirk valued his client. He wanted to help. But he knew that he needed to be authentic with her. He told her that she couldn't make a team out of people who don't want to be a team. You have to take the risk to say, "There's an elephant in the room." That's what team building is, and only by doing that will anything change. In this case Dirk had to be authentic and had to challenge his client to also be authentic—to take the risk. ◀

Another example of authenticity is shown in the next client story. But it is clear that the consultant also had to be inner-directed and value the uniqueness of her client's situation in order to be effective.

▶ SUCCESSION PLANNING

A short time ago Louise took on a new client who was looking for a new CEO. The initial meeting was with the board. The board knew of Louise's firm's work and thought she'd be more helpful than a search firm, as they wanted to look internally rather than externally. They wanted a leader who could truly make a difference. They liked the fact that Louise also helped further develop the leaders to go the distance once they were identified.

At the first meeting, the client detailed what needed to be done. They had a slate of internal candidates and an idea of which ones were the top candidates; Louise just needed to pick one. While having a slate of candidates was OK, Louise wanted to know how they arrived at their list. It was clear that they hadn't been through something like this before. If they wanted someone to anoint a candidate, Louise's firm was not the one for the job. Louise told them she needed to understand their firm, their needs, and each of the candidates.

They appreciated her authenticity, her inner-directedness, and the uniqueness she placed on their process and their firm; she was hired. The client came to understand as well that the selection process was critically important in determining who their next leader was. ◄

In the final example, the importance of self-acceptance and resiliency is illustrated.

► UNILATERAL VISION

All of us have had clients who don't listen. Recently Leslie had a client who had developed a new vision for his department. It was a great vision; Leslie liked it. However, it was too big a stretch for the department. Leslie felt the department needed a fair amount of work before it was able to set its heights so high. Leslie directly, albeit tactfully, tried to tell the client that his team wasn't supporting the vision. He needed greater buy-in. The client's message to Leslie was that he didn't care. He said that it was time "these people" were challenged. The only way to ensure success was by making a bold statement.

Not surprisingly, he didn't contract with Leslie for the work. Leslie struggled with it a little and second-guessed herself for the moment, but she'd taken the risk that she thought she should take. She practiced self-acceptance and resiliency and moved on. ◄

Reflections

In all these examples, you can see how consultants can leverage the drivers for success. Every consultant has at his or her disposal the creativity and risk-taking drivers we've discussed. Being more creative and taking more risks is what makes us better practitioners. It's what enables us to lead rather than follow and challenge rather than accept the status quo.

Is It Working?

There are a number of telltale signs that indicate the effectiveness of the innovation equation. While it is natural to ask, "How do I know whether this is working?" we've seen its success in the field and offer the following quick list of signals that success is beginning to take hold:

- People identify with and share their Creatrix orientation (as in, "I'm a Practicalizer");
- People discuss and share stories of what driver(s) they're working on (as in, "I'm really trying to be resilient because I had the following setbacks recently. . .");
- People take the risk to challenge one another on the drivers (as in, "Are you really being authentic now?");
- People are fostering, rather than squelching, the momentum when ideas are introduced;
- The organizational culture adopts more of a "can do" attitude;
- There is talk of stretching one's reach;
- The orientations and drivers are adopted into the language of meetings;
- People begin to see and believe in possibilities; and
- People are more tolerant of one another.

Final Thoughts

Our research tells us that individuals, teams, and organizations want to be known for innovation. Congratulations! You have just taken the first steps to building your innovative capacity. You now have the formula for innovation or, as we like to call it, the innovation equation. But don't stop here. If you do, this becomes just another book on the shelf that yields little in terms of actual business results. Unleash the creativity and risk taking within and begin to watch the innovative ideas flow.

We assume that, because you've read this far, you indeed have a real need for building innovative capacity. What you need to do now is build on your newfound knowledge. That is, take a risk! Get creative! In short, be innovative. We know it's easier said than done, but it's also just a matter of doing it!

Appendix A
I³: Investing in Innovation

THIS SIMULATION IS DESIGNED to combine the elements of risk taking and creativity to foster innovative results. The simulation requires teams of people to bet on their own ability to solve an abstract problem creatively. The game has two rounds. Learnings occur from debriefing the risk-taking culture of the groups and individuals within the groups, as well as by debriefing the creativity process (brainstorming, innovative processes, and so forth).

Number of Participants

Sixteen to twenty participants is ideal, although the game is easily modified for smaller or larger numbers. The participants are equally divided into two groups, and a few people in each group are assigned as observers.

Time

One and one-half hours (15 minutes for setup; 45 minutes on the tasks—15 minutes each for betting strategy, round one, and round two; and 30 minutes for debriefing—10 minutes each for risk taking, creativity, and innovation).

Rules and Process of the Simulation

Each group of players is given twenty chips. The goal of the game is to win *and* to not lose! In the event of a tie, both teams lose. The minimum bet is one chip, and the maximum bet is twenty chips. After the first round, each team that did not solve the problem is limited to wagering only what they bet in the first round (avoiding risk until you have experience is not risky and therefore not rewarded) and they can only wager what they have left. For example, if a team only bet one chip in the first round, then it can only bet one chip in the second round. If a team bets ten chips in the first round, it can bet ten chips in the second round. If a team bets eleven chips in the first round (and does not solve the problem), it can only wager nine chips in the second round. The groups are given time to calculate their wagers and to determine their collective risk-taking propensity. Then the individual groups are split into "Home Office" and "Field Reps" (subgroups of the same team). The Field Reps are given the following objects: a watch, a candy bar, a record, an iron, and a football (in that order) and sent out of the room (into the "field"). To win the game, the Home Office has to get the Field Reps to walk back into the room in the proper sequence. The correct sequence upon return is football, iron, record, candy bar, and watch. The Home Office is only allowed to communicate with the Field Reps by using "p-mail" (paper plane version of e-mail). A limit of two p-mails may be used each round (up to four total p-mails). The p-mails can only contain one word, which is audited by the facilitator. Each word must be an actual dictionary-defined word, must be written in all capital letters, and cannot contain any other markings. The team that enters the room from the field in the proper order and has wagered the most wins!

Solutions

What initially seems like a challenging problem is, in retrospect, quite easily solved with a little creative thinking. First, most groups (even with little creative effort) should be able to sequence the items in the proper order after using four one-word p-mails (simply list the football on the first p-mail, the iron on the second, and so on). However, enabling the Field Reps to re-enter in the right sequence the first time around requires "reframing the issue" (a popular creativity technique) to arrive at the proper solution. One potential solution is to have the first p-mail contain the word "ACRONYM." The second p-mail then contains the acronym "FIRST" (Football, Iron, Record, Sweets, and Timepiece). Now obviously, the football, iron, and record fall into place quite nicely for the Field Reps; the question remains, with two letters left will they reframe the candy bar to mean "sweets" and the watch to mean "time"? Another solution is to simply "RECALL" (word on the first p-mail) the items from the field and have them walk back in "REVERSE" (word on the second p-mail). This solution presumes that the items were given to the Field Reps in a particular order. Interestingly, this assumption as well as a host of other assumptions come into play during the simulation. The list of potential creative solutions is virtually unlimited.

Insights and Learnings
Risk Taking

There is an "optimum" appropriate risk-taking level (and, as in life, it is neither total risk aversion [one chip] nor flagrant risk [twenty chips]). Not knowing what the other team is betting is key to this risk-taking exercise. As in business, not knowing what the competition is up to is a major variable. Betting only one chip each round guarantees a team eighteen chips at the end, which may be enough to win, but it is a risk-adverse strategy that speaks volumes about the group's paradigms and confidence about being able to solve challenging problems! Betting ten chips or fewer in the first round will at best result in a tie if the other team bets the same number. Therefore, betting eleven chips (risking more than half of the chips in a two-round game) shows true risk taking and is the optimum level, as it indicates that the team wants to win, rather than tie. It also gives the team the greatest chance of success in the second round (with nine chips left, if they fail, they can still win eighteen chips total if they win in the second round after betting the remaining nine chips). Betting more than eleven chips may be considered too much risk for some, as it does not optimize the second round odds. Therefore, the optimum level is an eleven-chip bet. You will have the opportunity when the groups debrief to discuss risk strategy in detail with the participants. Just remember that the optimum risk level for a team is rarely low or high, but somewhere beyond the safe middle ground and usually not the same as individual risk-taking levels!

Creativity

In the solutions section, we identified three potential ways of solving this abstract problem; all seem rather logical and simple in hindsight. This is true of all creative solutions: In hindsight, they seem rather obvious. However, prior to solving a problem, finding the solution can seem daunting. The first answer is rather linear in its approach. It doesn't enable winning in the first round (and it isn't really a creative solution), but it does work to get the Field Reps back in the room with the objects in the correct order. In the second solution, reframing the problem and careful use of words on the p-mails provides the solution. We needn't articulate too much about creatively "reframing the problem" here to make our point; this is one of the most widely accepted methods of creative problem solving. In the third answer, had the groups just paused long enough to maintain the original order in which they were sent out of the room, they would simply have to re-enter (as if they were being recalled) to have the correct sequence. Many times the creative solutions are right under our noses; all we need to do is pause and reflect a moment before we make a mountain out of a molehill.

Innovation

The concept of innovation is a function of risk taking and creativity. By definition, innovation is the act of introducing something new. Creative solutions are born in environments where risk is present. Risk creates pressure and a sense of urgency. Without risk, creativity often remains fodder for the dreamer. On the other hand, risk without creativity (ideas) is simply thrill seeking and rarely helps move people or teams forward. Creativity and risk taking together equal innovation! Only this combination of risk taking (betting on yourself to win) and creativity (new ideas) creates the right environment and maximum results in order to win (both in the simulation and in today's world). Innovation is what many of today's organizations need to stay competitive and resolve difficult business issues.

Additional Comments

The goal of this simulation is to observe *individual and team* risk-taking and creativity dynamics. By definition, individuals and teams should and will struggle with the basic constructs. That is, they will be required to bet (on themselves and against the competition) on their ability to solve an unknown problem. This means taking a risk and being creative in an intentionally ambiguous environment. Resist attempts to bring clarity (thereby reducing ambiguity) to the situation. Further, resist attempts to moderate betting strategies. Simply allow the teams the opportunity to struggle with their varying tolerances for risk and creativity.

Initial communication regarding the constructs of the game should be made to the whole group at large before disbanding into teams. Make every attempt to limit clarifying questions at the team level (thereby giving some teams an unintentional advantage). Do not allow teams to witness or observe the other team's betting or problem-solving strategies. Having observers simply watch the simulation (when group size permits) provides insights to the individuals and teams from an outsider's perspective, which is often quite different.

Debriefing the Simulation

Debrief the simulation first on the risk-taking construct (betting strategies), then on the creativity construct (solving the problem), and finally on innovation in general. Table A.1 provides a sample list of discussion questions to help you start and sustain your debriefing session.

Table A.1. Sample Discussion Questions

Topic	Questions
Risk Taking	How did you arrive at the number of chips your team wagered?
	Was everybody on the team comfortable with this strategy?
	Who went along with the team even though they may have wanted to wager a different strategy?
Creativity	What idea-generating strategies did your group employ?
	How did the team treat various ideas (for example, encouragement, dismissal, and so forth)?
	What assumptions did the team make?
Innovation	What, if anything, prevented you from being fully creative or taking risks?
	How did "group think" affect individual creativity and risk taking?
	How was this simulation similar to innovation in organizations today?

Participant Handouts

The handouts on the following pages should be used to guide the participants through the simulation. It is important to distribute these materials only to the intended recipients; otherwise the simulation will be compromised. Table A.2 indicates to whom the materials should be distributed.

Table A.2. Distribution of Handouts

Title	Distribution
Overview	All participants
Instructions for Home Office	Home Office only
Instructions for Field Reps	Field Reps only
Instructions for Observers	Observers only
Observer's Notepad	Observers only
Objects to Be Sequenced	Home Office only
P-Mail	Home Office only
Debriefing Notepad	All participants

Overview
Objective

The objective is to win the game! In the event of a tie, both teams lose. The first team to solve the problem correctly wins the game. If no teams solve the problem or both teams solve the problem in the same round, the team that bets the most "chips" wins the game! *The object is to get the Field Reps to sequence a group of unrelated items with very limited communication from the Home Office.*

Teams

Teams will be subdivided into two smaller groups as the game progresses. Several team members will stay in the room and be referred to as the "Home Office." Several other people will leave the room and be referred to as "Field Reps." Some observers will also be selected.

Betting

This simulation potentially involves two rounds. *The second round is necessary if neither team wins in the first round.* Betting occurs before the beginning of each round. Each team begins with twenty chips. The minimum bet is one chip. The maximum bet is twenty chips. After the first round, each team that did not solve the problem is limited to wagering only what it bet in the first round. Each team is limited to wagering only the amount of money it has available. For example, if a team only bets one chip in the first round, then it can only bet one chip in the second round. If a team bets ten chips in the first round, then it can bet ten chips in the second round. If a team bets eleven chips in the first round, it can only wager nine chips in the second round. Each team will be given time to calculate betting strategies.

Instructions for Home Office

Your job is to get the Field Reps to sequence the group of items in the order that you are instructed. You will be able to communicate with your Field Reps via p-mail (plane-mail, a paper plane version of e-mail). You will be able to send up to two one-word p-mails (per round) to help guide your Field Reps in sequencing the objects.

A Word or Two About P-Mail

- Only one word can be written on the P-mail.

- The word must be written in all CAPITAL letters.

- The word must be a dictionary-defined word (no acronyms allowed!).

- To ensure compliance, the facilitators will audit each p-mail.

- No other type of communication is allowed (symbols, gestures, pictures).

Instructions for Field Reps

Your job is simply to sequence the group of items in the order that the Home Office desires. The Home Office will communicate with you via p-mail (plane-mail, a paper plane version of e-mail). You will get up to two one-word p-mails (per round) to help you sequence the objects.

A Word or Two About P-Mail

- Only one word can be written on the P-mail.

- The word must be written in all CAPITAL letters.

- The word must be a dictionary-defined word (no acronyms allowed!).

- To ensure compliance, the facilitators will audit each p-mail.

- No other type of communication is allowed (symbols, gestures, pictures).

Instructions for Observers

Your job is to observe the teams in action. Some may be assigned to observe just the "Home Office" people and others may be assigned to observe just the "Field Reps." In either case, your goal is to document your observations (paying particular attention to risk-taking and creativity actions). Document words, phrases, and behaviors that either support or discourage risk taking and creativity.

Helpful Hints

- Observe all behaviors, both verbal (intonation, tone, pitch, stress, and so forth) and nonverbal (posture, facial expressions, and so on).

- Look for as many risk-taking and creativity behaviors as possible.

Gentle Reminders

- Document as many observations as possible to support your views.

- *DO NOT identify specific individuals in your observations.*

Observer's Notepad

Risk-Taking Observations:

_____
_____
_____
_____
_____
_____
_____
_____
_____
_____
_____
_____
_____

Creativity Observations:

_____
_____
_____
_____
_____
_____
_____
_____
_____
_____
_____
_____
_____
_____

Objects to Be Sequenced

The objects and their proper sequence:

1. Football
2. Iron
3. Record
4. Candy Bar
5. Watch

P-Mail: Paper Plane Version of E-Mail

Fold this sheet into a paper airplane.

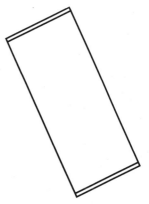

Debriefing Notepad

Insights on Risk Taking:

_____
_____
_____
_____
_____
_____
_____
_____

Insights on Creativity:

_____
_____
_____
_____
_____
_____
_____
_____

Lessons in Innovation:

_____
_____
_____
_____
_____
_____
_____
_____

Appendix B
The Creatrix Ba: A Process for Creating Innovative Ideas

THE CREATRIX BA is a simple, yet powerful process for creating innovative ideas in teams.

The Roots of the Process

First, it is important to understand the concept of Ba. Ba is a Japanese word essentially defined as "a shared space for emerging relationships" (Nonaka & Konno, 1998). This incredibly powerful method for creating ideas came about through a combination of different methods we were using: brainstorming, role playing, T-group theory, and the C&RT laboratory work of Richard Byrd (1974). Combining these methods with the understanding of Ba led to our drivers of innovation.

The Importance of Developing an Aim

To begin with, it is important to develop an agreed on aim in the group. The aim is used to define a goal or an objective for innovation. For example, innovations for a specific customer service focus, innovation for new product ideas, and so on. The idea is to build the innovative capacity of individuals and teams around specific aims. Aims are essential for developing innovative ideas. Coupling an aim with the seven drivers of innovation makes it possible to increase the capacity for greater innovation.

Now, armed with this understanding you are ready to capture the essence of the Creatrix Ba.

Steps in the Process

1. Determine the innovative aim for the group. You can have members of the team call out problems or issues or tasks that they want to develop innovative ideas for. Select one to focus on.

2. Have the group move into a circle facing in. There should be no barriers such as tables or desks—just people sitting in a circle facing each other.

3. Write the aim on a large piece of newsprint, overhead transparency, or some other medium.

4. Place this written aim in the center of a circle of people.

5. Inform the group in the circle that they have an hour [you need at least one hour] to generate as many completely new ideas as they can to accomplish this aim.

6. Their charge: In the hour allotted they must develop at least three new ideas to address the aim. These must be *brand new ideas* that no one has heard of before.

7. And here is one of the most important messages—*no one can talk during this hour.*

8. Tell them they're on their own and that you will not answer any more questions for the next hour. Leave the group with this intentionally ambiguous situation. Simply encourage the group to complete the task at hand given the prescribed rules. They must figure out the process to do this.

9. Sit back and let the process take over. They will create more ideas than they or you imagined were possible.

Note: They will initially struggle with how they are going to come up with the ideas and share them. Usually, someone will grab a flip chart. They will also struggle with how to indicate those ideas they've heard before—being especially conscious of not hurting someone's feelings. They will figure out unique ways to get over these obstacles. Usually, they will start listing ideas and someone in the group will come up and cross off an idea. This creates greater momentum in the group to succeed. Make sure supplies (such as a flip chart and markers or an overhead projector and blank transparencies) are available, but do not direct them to use these resources. Don't give them any other direction than what's noted above.

The Debriefing

This process creates a dynamic in which every driver can come alive and gives everyone an opportunity to see the importance of creating a culture in which the drivers become the dominant operant for building greater innovation. These are listed below.

Creativity Drivers

- There's ambiguity in the situation—minimal constraints and guidance;
- There's independence—no one can look to someone else for direction;
- There's inner directedness—what do I offer to the Ba in terms of ideas or processes, without fear of retribution, ridicule, or judgment; and
- There's uniqueness—each person believes in the uniqueness of his or her ideas and is simply left to ponder the beauty of others' ideas.

Risk-Taking Drivers

- There's authenticity—people just submit their ideas, without opportunity for grand explanations;
- There's resiliency—people learn to share more ideas as other ideas are crossed out; and finally
- There's self-acceptance—no one can make you feel bad about the ideas you submit.

The Creatrix Ba creates a power in the room unlike anything we've ever experienced. Use the following questions to drive a discussion about the participants' experience:

- What's behind this unique experience?
- Is it the silence?

- Is it focusing on your own driver?
- Is it the amount of time allowed?
- Is it the aim and the focus?
- Is it the rhythm that develops?
- Is it the tacit understandings?
- Is it the circle (with no barriers)?
- Is it the Creatrix Ba itself?

It is each of these variables in different forms that make the Creatrix Ba the most powerful tool for generating innovative ideas today.

Bibliography

Agor, W.H. (1991). How intuition can be used to enhance creativity in organizations. *Journal of Creative Behavior, 25*(1), 11–18.

Allport, G. (1955). *Becoming.* New Haven, CT: Yale University Press.

Amabile, T.M. (1996, January 23). The motivation for creativity in organizations. *Harvard Business Review On Point.* Boston, MA: Harvard Business School. No. 9–396–240.

Amabile, T.M. (1998, September/October). How to kill creativity. *Harvard Business Review On Point.* Boston, MA: Harvard Business School.

Amabile, T.M. (2001, April). Beyond talent, John Irving and the passionate craft of creativity. *American Psychologist, 56*(4), 333–336.

American heritage dictionary (3rd ed.). (1994). New York: Houghton Mifflin.

Anderson, W. (1988). *The greatest risk of all.* New York: Houghton Mifflin.

Armenakis, A.A., Harris, S.G., & Mossholder, K.W. (1993). Creating readiness for organizational change. *Human Relations, 46*(6).

Badaracco, J.L., Jr. (1997). *Defining moments.* Boston, MA: Harvard Business School Press.

Bailin, S. (1992). *Achieving extraordinary ends.* Norwood, NJ: Abex.

Bennis, W. (1993). *An invented life.* Reading, MA: Addison-Wesley.

Bennis, W., & Nanus, B. (1985). *Leaders: Strategies for taking charge.* New York: Harper & Row.

Biolos, J. (1996). Six steps toward making a team innovative. *Harvard Management Update,* No. U9608C.

Boone, L.E., & Kurtz, D.L. (1982). *Contemporary business* (3rd ed.). New York: Dryden.

Bridges, W. (1991). *Making transitions: Making the most of change.* San Francisco, CA: Perseus.

Bruner, J.S. (1960). *The process of education.* Cambridge, MA: Harvard University Press.

Byrd, J.L. (1998, April 6). Risk-taking is essential for businesses to stay competitive. *Minneapolis Star Tribune,* p. D3.

Bryd, J.L. (2000). *Creatrix inventory instructions* [On-line]. Available: Creatrix website, www.creatrix.com. Minneapolis, MN: Richard Byrd Company.

Byrd, J.L., & Brown, P.L. (2001). Two leadership basics: Creativity and risk taking. *OD Practitioner, 35*(4), 41–44.

Byrd, R.E. (1968, November). Redressing the balance with creative risk taking training. *Adult Leadership.*

Byrd, R.E. (1970). *Self actualization through creative risk taking: A new laboratory model.* Unpublished doctoral dissertation. New York: New York University Press.

Byrd, R.E. (1971, May). How much risk can you afford to take? *Management Review.*

Byrd, R.E. (1973). Self actualization through creative risk taking. In D.W. Johnson (Ed.), *Contemporary social psychology.* New York: J.B. Lippincott.

Byrd, R.E. (1974). *A guide to personal risk taking.* New York: AMACOM.

Byrd, R.E. (1975, June). Daring to be different. *Industry Week.* Also in L.J. Loudenback (Ed.). (1976). *Student manual of practical marketing.* Santa Monica, CA: Goodyear.

Byrd, R.E. (1982). *Managing risks in changing times.* Basking Ridge, NJ: American Telephone & Telegraph.

Bryd, R.E. (1971, 1982, 1986). *C&RT.* San Francisco, CA: Jossey-Bass/Pfeiffer.

Byrd, R.E. (1994, March-April). Five risk-taking exercises for "nice girls." *Executive Female, 12*(2).

Byrd, R.E., & Byrd, J.L. (1988). Uncertainty and risk taking. In J.W. Pfeiffer (Ed.), *The 1988 annual: Developing human resources.* San Francisco, CA: Jossey-Bass/Pfeiffer.

Calvert, G. (1993). *Highwire management.* San Francisco, CA: Jossey-Bass.

Carr, N.G. (1999, September-October). Visualizing innovation. *Harvard Business Review.*

Chesbrough, H.W., & Teece, D.J. (1996, January-February). When is virtual virtuous? Organizing for innovation. *Harvard Business Review.*

Christensen, C.M. (2000). *The innovator's dilemma.* Boston, MA: Harvard Business School.

Christensen, C.M., & Overdorf, M. (2001). Meeting the challenge of disruptive change. *Harvard Business Review on Innovation,* pp. 103–129.

Covey, S.R. (1989). *The seven habits of highly effective people.* New York: Fireside.

Cox, C. (1926). *Genetic studies of genius, Vol. II. The early mental traits of three hundred geniuses.* Stanford, CA: Stanford University.

Csikszentmihalyi, M. (1975). *Beyond boredom and anxiety.* San Francisco, CA: Jossey-Bass.

Csikszentmihalyi, M. (1988). Society, culture and person: A systems view of creativity. In R.J. Sternberg (Ed.), *The nature of creativity.* Cambridge, MA: Cambridge University.

Csikszentmihalyi, M. (1990). The domain of creativity. In M.A. Runco & R.S. Albert (Eds.), *Theories of creativity.* Thousand Oaks, CA: Sage.

Dawson, R. (1993). *The confident decision maker.* New York: William Morrow.

de Bono, E. (1973). *Lateral thinking: Creativity step by step.* New York: Harper.

de Bono, E. (1985). *Six thinking hats.* Boston, MA: Little, Brown.

Deal, T.E., & Kennedy, A.A. (1982). *Corporate cultures.* Reading, MA: Addison-Wesley.

Deci, E.L., & Ryan, R.M. (1985). *Intrinsic motivation and self-determination in human behavior.* New York: Plenum.

DePree, M. (1993). *Leadership jazz.* New York: Doubleday.

Drucker, P.F. (1985, May-June). The discipline of innovation. *Harvard Business Review.*

Drucker, P.F., Dyson, E., Handy, C., Saffo, P., & Senge, P.M. (1997, September-October). Looking ahead: Implications of the present. *Harvard Business Review,* pp. 18–32.

Dudik, E.M. (1993). *Strategic renaissance.* New York: AMACOM.

Dym, B., & Hutson, H. (1997). Utilizing states of organizational readiness. *OD Practitioner, 29*(2), 32–43.

Emshoff, J.R., & Denlinger, T.E. (1992). *The new rules of the game: The four key experiences managers must have to thrive in the non-hierarchical 90s and beyond.* New York: Harper Business.

Essex, L., & Kusy, M. (1999). *Fast forward leadership.* London: Biddles Ltd., Guilford & Kings Lynn.

Foster, R., & Kaplan, S. (2001). *Creative destruction.* New York: Doubleday.

Fritz, R. (1991). *Creating.* New York: Fawcett Columbine.

Fromm, E. (1947). *Man for himself.* New York: Fawcett.

Fromm, E. (1971). *Escape from freedom.* New York: Avon.

Garfield, C. (1986). *Peak performers.* New York: William Morrow.

Gelb, M.J. (1998). *How to think like Leonardo da Vinci.* New York: Dell.

Godfrey, J. (1992). *Our wildest dreams: Women entrepreneurs making money, having fun, doing good.* New York: HarperCollins.

Godin, S. (2000, August). Unleash your idea virus. *Fast Company,* pp. 115–135.

Goleman, D. (1995). *Emotional intelligence.* New York: Bantam.

Gruber, H.E., & Wallace, D.B. (2001, April). Creative work. *American Psychologist, 56*(4), 346–349.

Hamel, G. (2000, June 12). Reinvent your company. *Fortune,* pp. 99–112.

Hamel, G., & Prahalad, C.K. (1994). *Competing for the future.* Boston, MA: Harvard Business School Press.

Handy, C. (1996). *Beyond certainty.* Boston, MA: Harvard Business School Press.

Hargadon, A., & Sutton, R.I. (2001). Building an innovation factory. In *Harvard Business Review On Point Collection, Continuous Innovation: No Genius Required,* pp. 3–17.

Herzberg, F. (1966). *Work and the nature of man.* Cleveland, OH: World Publishing.

Higgins, J. (1995). *Innovate or evaporate.* Winter Park, FL: New Management.

Hippel, E., Thomke, S., & Sonnack, M. (1999, September-October). Creating breakthroughs at 3M. *Harvard Business Review,* pp. 47–57.

Hirshberg, J. (1998). *The creative priority. Driving innovative business in the real world.* New York: HarperCollins.

Iacovini, J. (1993, January). The human side of organization change. *Training & Development, 65*(4).

Jeffers, S. (1988). *Feel the fear and do it anyway.* New York: Ballantine.

Kanter, R.M.(1983). *The change masters.* New York: Simon & Schuster.

Kao, J. (1990). *The entrepreneurial organization.* Upper Saddle River, NJ: Prentice Hall.

Kehrer, D. (1989). *Doing business boldly: Essential lessons in the art of taking intelligent risks.* New York: Simon & Schuster.

Kelley, T., with Littman, J. (2001). *The art of innovation: Lessons in creativity from IDEO, America's leading design firm.* New York: Doubleday Broadway.

Keyes, R. (1985). *Chancing it (Why we take risks).* Boston, MA: Little, Brown.

Kim, W.C., & Mauborgne, R. (1999). Value innovation: The strategic logic of high growth. In *Harvard Business Review on Breakthrough Thinking,* pp. 189–217.

Kogan, N., & Wallach, M.A. (1964). *Risk taking: A study in cognition and personality.* Westport, CT: Greenwood.

Kotter, J.P. (1996). *Leading change.* Boston, MA: Harvard Business School Press.

Kouzes, J.M., & Posner, B.Z. (1987). *The leadership challenge: How to get extraordinary things done in organizations.* San Francisco, CA: Jossey-Bass.

Kriegel, R.J., & Patler, L. (1991). *If it ain't broke—break it: And other unconditional wisdom for a changing business world.* New York: Warner.

Landrum, G.N. (1993). *Profiles of genius.* Buffalo, NY: Prometheus.

Leider, R.J. (1999). *On purpose: A journal about taking charge of your life/work.* Minneapolis, MN: The Inventure Group.

Leider, R.J., & Shapiro, D.A. (1996). *Repacking your bags: Lighten your load for the rest of your life.* San Francisco, CA: Berrett-Koehler.

Leonard, D. (1998, Spring). The role of tacit knowledge in group innovation. *California Management Review, 40*(3), 112–132.

Leonard, D., & Rayport, J.F. (1997, November-December). Spark innovation through empathic design. *Harvard Business Review,* pp. 102–113.

Leonard, D., & Straus, S. (1999). Putting your company's whole brain to work. In *Harvard Business Review on Breakthrough Thinking,* pp. 57–85.

Maroosis, J. (2001). How to anticipate and capitalize on innovation. *Harvard Management Update.* No. U0101D.

Martindale, C. (2001, April). Oscillations and analogies. *American Psychologist, 56*(4), 342–345.

Maslow, A.H. (1962). *Toward a psychology of being.* New York: D. Van Nostrand.

May, R. (1961). *Existential psychology.* New York: Random House.

Miller, L.M. (1989). *Barbarians to bureaucrats.* New York: Fawcett Columbine.

Nakamura, J., & Csikszentmihalyi, M. (2001, April). Catalytic creativity. *American Psychologist, 56*(4), 337–341.

Nonaka, I., & Konno, N. (1998, Spring). The concept of "ba." *California Management Review, 40*(3), 40–54.

O'Connor, G.C., & Rice, M.P. (2001, Winter). Opportunity recognition and breakthrough innovation in large established firms. *California Management Review, 43*(2), 95–116.

Pascale, R., Millemann, M., & Gioja, L. (1997, November-December). Changing the way we change. *Harvard Business Review,* pp. 126–139.

Peters, T. (1987). *Thriving on chaos.* New York: Alfred A. Knopf.

Peters, T. (1995, June 5). A nation of wimps. *Forbes, 152* (2).

Peters, T. (1997). *The circle of innovation.* New York: Alfred A. Knopf.

Popcorn, F., & Marigold, L. (1996). *Clicking.* New York: HarperCollins.

PricewaterhouseCoopers. (2000). *Innovation and growth: A global perspective* [On-line]. Available: pwcglobal.com

Quade, K., & Brown, R. (2002). *The conscious consultant.* San Francisco, CA: Jossey-Bass/Pfeiffer.

Quinn, J.B. (1985, May-June). Managing innovation: Controlled chaos. *Harvard Business Review.*

Quinn, J.B., Anderson, P., & Finkelstein, S. (1996, March-April). Managing professional intellect: Making the most of the best. *Harvard Business Review,* pp. 71–80.

Quinn, R.E., Hildebrandt, H.W., Rogers, P., & Thompson, M. P. (1991). A competing values framework for analyzing presentational communication in management contexts. *The Journal of Business Communication, 28*(3), 213–231.

Riesman, D. (1950). *The lonely crowd.* New York: Doubleday.

Robinson, A.G., & Stern, S. (1998). *Corporate creativity. How innovation and improvement actually happen.* San Francisco, CA: Berrett-Koehler.

Rogers, C. (1961). *On becoming a person.* Boston, MA: Houghton Mifflin.

Rogers, E.M. (1995). *Diffusion of innovations* (4th ed.). New York: The Free Press.

Roweton, W.E. (1989). Enhancing individual creativity in American business and education. *Journal of Creative Behavior, 23*(4), 248–256.

Runco, M.A., & Okuda, S.M. (1988). Problem-discovery, divergent thinking, and the creative process. *Journal of Youth and Adolescence, 17,* 211–220.

Schrage, M. (1999). Faster innovation? Try rapid prototyping. *Harvard Management Update,* No. U9912D.

Shapira, Z. (1995). *Risk taking: A managerial perspective.* New York: Russell Sage Foundation.

Sittenfeld, C. (2000, June). The most creative man in Silicon Valley. *Fast Company,* pp. 274–292.

Smith, D.K. (1996). *Taking charge of change.* Reading, MA: Addison-Wesley.

Sternberg, R.J. (2001, April). What is the common thread of creativity? *American Psychologist, 56*(4), 360–362.

Sternberg, R.J., & Dess, N.K. (2001, April). Creativity for the new millennium. *American Psychologist, 56*(4), 332.

Stevens, B. (1996, January). Using the competing values framework to assess corporate ethical codes. *The Journal of Business Communication, 33*(1).

Stokes, P.D. (2001, April). Variability, constraints, and creativity. *American Psychologist, 56*(4), 355–359.

Sturner, W. (1990). *Calculated risk: Strategies for managing change.* Buffalo, NY: Bearly.

Taylor, W.C. (2000, October). You say you want a revolution. *Fast Company,* pp. 90–94.

Thomke, S. (2001). Enlightened experimentation: The new imperative for innovation. *Harvard Business Review On Point Collection, Continuous Innovation: No Genius Required,* pp. 33–47.

Thorpe, S. (2000). *How to think like Einstein.* Naperville, IL: Sourcebooks.

Tillich, P.F. (1957). *Dynamics of faith.* New York: Harper Brothers.

Torrance, P. (Ed.). (1959). Creativity. *Proceedings of the Second Minnesota Conference on Gifted Children.* Minneapolis, MN: University of Minnesota, Center for Continuation Study.

Tushman, M.L., & O'Reilly, C.A., III. (1997). *Winning through innovation.* Boston, MA: Harvard Business School Press.

Viscott, D. (1977). *Risking.* New York: Simon & Schuster.

Ward, T.B. (2001, April). Creative cognition, conceptual combination, and the creative writing of Stephen R. Donaldson. *American Psychologist, 56*(4), 350–354.

Whyte, D. (1994). *The heart aroused.* New York: Currency Doubleday.

Winslow, E.K. (1990). The issue of motivating entre(intra)preneurial behavior. *Journal of Creative Behavior, 24*(4), 256–261.

Zipes, J. (Trans.). (1987). *The complete fairy tales of the brothers Grimm.* New York: Bantam.

About the Series

THERE ARE WATERSHED MOMENTS in history that change everything after them. The attack on Pearl Harbor was one of those. The bombing of Hiroshima was another. The terrorist attack on the World Trade Center in New York City was our most recent. All resulted in significant change that transformed many lives and organizations.

Practicing Organization Development: The Change Agent Series for Groups and Organizations was launched to help those who must cope with or create change. The series is designed to share what is working or not working, to provoke critical thinking about change, and to offer creative ways to deal with change, rather than the destructive ones noted above.

The Current State of Change Management and Organization Development

Almost as soon as the ink was dry on the first wave of books published in this series, we heard that its focus was too narrow. We heard that the need for theory and practice extended beyond OD into change management. More than one respected authority urged us to reconsider our focus, moving beyond OD to include books on change management generally.

Organization development is not the only way that change can be engineered or coped with in organizational settings. We always knew that, of course. And we remain grounded in the view that change management, however it is carried out, should be based on such values as respect for the individual, participation and involvement in change by those affected by it, and interest in the improvement of organizational settings on many levels—including productivity improvement, but also improvement in achieving work/life balance and in a values-based approach to management and to change.

A Brief History of the Genesis of the Series

A few years ago, and as a direct result of the success of *Practicing Organization Development: A Guide for Practitioners* by Rothwell, Sullivan, and McLean, the publisher—feeling that OD was experiencing a rebirth of interest in the United States and in other nations—wanted to launch a new OD series. The goal of this new series was not to replace, or even compete directly with, the well-established Addison-Wesley OD Series (edited by Edgar Schein). Instead, as the editors saw it, the series would provide a means by which the most promising authors in OD whose voices had not previously been heard could share their ideas. The publisher enlisted the support of Bill Rothwell, Roland Sullivan, and Kristine Quade to turn the dream of a series into a reality.

This series was long in the making and has been steadily evolving since its inception. The original vision was an ambitious one—and involved no less than reinventing OD and re-energizing interest in the research and practice surrounding it. Sponsoring books was one means to that end. Another is the series website (www.pfeiffer.com/go/od). Far more than just a place to advertise the series, it serves as a real-time learning community for OD practitioners.

What Distinguishes the Books in this Series

The books in this series are meant to be challenging, cutting-edge, and state-of-the-art in their approach to OD and change management. The goal of the series is to provide an outlet for proven authorities in OD and change management who have not put their ideas into print or for up-and-coming writers in OD and change management who have new, sometimes unorthodox, approaches that are stimulating and exciting. Some books in this series describe inspirational concepts that can lead to actionable change and purvey ideas so new that they are not fully developed.

Unique to this series is the cutting-edge emphasis, the immediate applicability, and the ease of transferability of the concepts. The aim of this series is nothing less than to reinvent, re-energize, and reinvigorate OD and change management. In each book, we have also recommended that the author(s) provide:

- A research base of some kind, meaning new information derived from practice and/or systematic investigation and

- Practical tools, worksheets, case studies, and other ready-to-go approaches that help the authors drag "theory" to "practice" to make these new, cutting-edge approaches more concrete.

Subject Matter That Will (and Will Not) Be Covered

The books in this series are varied in their approach, but they are united by their focus. All share an emphasis on organization development (OD) and change management (CM). Hence, books in this series are about participative change efforts. They are not about such other popular topics as leadership, management development, consulting, or group dynamics—unless those topics are treated in new, cutting-edge ways and are geared to OD and change management practitioners.

This Book

Deep down within each of us lies the capacity to innovate. As individuals, we have an unknown and virtually unlimited capacity for creativity and risk taking. Learning how to unleash these drivers of innovation creates unique personal expression and powerful business results. Through greater understanding of creativity and risk taking, greater innovation is possible.

The Innovation Equation presents an exciting possibility for growth. Organizations, teams, and individuals can learn to tap into the creative and risk-taking capacity of individuals to make innovation possible. The authors have studied organizations where innovation occurs. They've identified, captured, analyzed, described, and celebrated people who are innovators. Now, more importantly, the authors can show you how to deliberately create it.

William J. Rothwell
University Park, PA

Roland Sullivan
Deephaven, MN

Kristine Quade
Minnetonka, MN

Statement
of the Board

①T IS OUR PLEASURE TO PARTICIPATE in and influence the start-up of *Practicing Organization Development: The Change Agent Series for Groups and Organizations.* The purpose of the series is to stimulate the profession and influence how organization change is defined and practiced. This statement is intended to set the context for the series by addressing three important questions: (1) What are the key issues facing organization change and development in the 21st Century? (2) Where does—or should—OD fit in the field of organization change and development? and (3) What is the purpose of this series?

What Are the Key Issues Facing Organization Change and Development in the 21st Century?

One of the questions is the extent to which leaders can control forces or can only be reactive. Will globalization and external forces be so powerful that they will prevent organizations from being able to "stay ahead of the change curve"? And

175

what will be the role of technology, especially information technology, in the change process? To what extent can it be a carrier of change (as well as a source of change)?

What will the relationship be between imposed change and collaborative change? Will the increased education of the workforce demand the latter, or will the requirement of having to make fundamental changes demand leadership that sets goals that participants would not willingly set on their own? And what is the relationship between these two forms of change?

Who will be the change agent? Is this a separate profession, or will that increasingly be the responsibility of the organization's leaders? If the latter, how does that change the role of the change professional?

What will be the role of values for change in the 21st Century? Will the key values be performance—efficiency and effectiveness? And what role will the humanistic values of more traditional OD play? Or will the growth of knowledge (and human competence) as an organization's core competence make this a moot point in that performance can only occur if one takes account of humanistic values?

What is the relationship between other fields and the area of change? Can any change process that is not closely linked with strategy be truly effective? Can change agents focus only on process, or do they need to be knowledgeable and actively involved in the organization's products/services and understand the market niche in which the organization operates?

Where Does—or Should—OD Fit in the Field of Organization Change and Development?

We offer the following definition of OD to stimulate debate:

> Organization development is a system-wide and values-based collaborative process of applying behavioral science knowledge to the adaptive development, improvement, and reinforcement of such organizational features as the strategies, structures, processes, people, and cultures that lead to organization effectiveness.

The definition suggests that OD can be understood in terms of its several foci:

First, *OD is a system-wide process.* It works with whole systems. In the past, the bias has been toward working at the individual and group levels. More recently, the focus has shifted to organizations and multi-organization systems. We support that trend in general, but honor and acknowledge the fact that the traditional focus on smaller systems is both legitimate and necessary.

Second, *OD is values-based*. Traditionally, OD has attempted to distinguish itself from other forms of planned change and applied behavioral science by promoting a set of humanistic values and by emphasizing the importance of personal growth as a key to its practice. Today, that focus is blurred and there is much debate about the value base underlying the practice of OD. We support a more formal and direct conversation about what these values are and how the field is related to them.

Third, *OD is collaborative*. Our first value commitment as OD practitioners is to bring about an inclusive, diverse workforce with a focus of integrating differences into a world-wide culture mentality.

Fourth, *OD is based on behavioral science knowledge*. Organization development should incorporate and apply knowledge from sociology, psychology, anthropology, technology, and economics toward the end of making systems more effective. We support the continued emphasis in OD on behavioral science knowledge and believe that OD practitioners should be widely read and comfortable with several of the disciplines.

Fifth, *OD is concerned with the adaptive development, improvement, and reinforcement of strategies, structures, processes, people, culture, and other features of organizational life.* This statement describes not only the organizational elements that are the target of change but also the process by which effectiveness is increased. That is, OD works in a variety of areas, and it is focused on improving those areas. We believe that such a statement of process and content strongly implies that a key feature of OD is the transference of knowledge and skill to the system so that it is more able to handle and manage change in the future.

Sixth and finally, *OD is about improving organization effectiveness*. It is not just about making people happy; it is also concerned with meeting financial goals, improving productivity, and addressing stakeholder satisfaction. We believe that OD's future is closely tied to the incorporation of this value in its purpose and the demonstration of this objective in its practice.

This definition raises a host of questions:

- Are OD and organization change and development one and the same, or are they different?

- Has OD become just a collection of tools, methods, and techniques? Has it lost its values?

- Does it talk "systems," but ignore them in practice?
- Are consultants facilitators of change or activists of change?
- To what extent should consulting be driven by consultant value versus holding only the value of increasing the client's effectiveness?
- How can OD practitioners help formulate strategy, shape the strategy development process, contribute to the content of strategy, and drive how strategy will be implemented?
- How can OD focus on the drivers of change external to individuals, such as the external environment, business strategy, organization change, and culture change, as well as on the drivers of change internal to individuals, such as individual interpretations of culture, behavior, style, and mindset?
- How much should OD be part of the competencies of all leaders? How much should it be the sole domain of professionally trained, career-oriented OD practitioners?

What Is the Purpose of This Series?

This series is intended to provide current thinking about organization change and development as a field and to provide practical approaches based on sound theory and research. It is targeted for full-time external or internal change practitioners; top executives in charge of enterprise-wide change; and managers, HR practitioners, training and development professionals, and others who have responsibility for change in organizational and trans-organizational settings. At the same time, these books will be directed toward cutting-edge thinking and state-of-the-art approaches. In some cases, the ideas, approaches, or techniques described are still evolving, so the books are intended to open up dialogue.

We know that the books in this series will provide a leading forum for thought-provoking dialogue within the field.

About the Board Members

David Bradford is senior lecturer in organizational behavior at the Graduate School of Business, Stanford University, Palo Alto, California. He is co-author (with Allan R. Cohen) of *Managing for Excellence, Influence Without Authority,* and *POWER UP: Transforming Organizations Through Shared Leadership.*

W. Warner Burke is professor of psychology and education in the department of organization and leadership at Teachers College at Columbia University in New York. He also serves as a senior advisor to PricewaterhouseCoopers. His most recent publication is *Business Profiles of Climate Shifts: Profiles of Change Makers*, with William Trahant and Richard Koonce.

Edith Whitfield Seashore is an organization consultant and co-founder (with Morley Segal) of AUNTL Masters Program in Organization Development. She is co-author of *What Did You Say?* and *The Art of Giving and Receiving Feedback* and co-editor of *The Promise of Diversity.*

Robert Tannenbaum is emeritus professor of development of human systems, Graduate School of Management, University of California, Los Angeles, and recipient of the Lifetime Achievement Award by the National OD Network. He has published numerous books, including *Human Systems Development* (with Newton Margulies and Fred Massarik).

Christopher G. Worley is director, MSOD Program, Pepperdine University, Malibu, California. He is co-author of *Organization Development and Change* (7th ed.), with Tom Cummings, and of *Integrated Strategic Change*, with David Hitchin and Walter Ross.

Shaolin Zhang is senior manager of organization development for Motorola (China) Electronics Ltd. He received his master's degree in American Studies from Beijing Foreign Studies University, Beijing, China, and holds a Ph.D. in sociology from York University, Toronto, Ontario.

Afterword
to the Series
by Richard Beckhard

ON **1967,** Warren Bennis, Ed Schein, and I were faculty members of the Sloan School of Management at MIT. We decided to produce a series of paperback books that collectively would describe the state of the field of organization development (OD). Organization development as a field had been named by me and several others from our pioneer change effort at General Mills in Minneapolis, Minnesota, some ten years earlier.

Today I define OD as "a systemic and systematic change effort, using behavioral science knowledge and skill, to transform the organization to a new state."

In any case, several books and many articles had been written, but there was no consensus on whether OD was a field of practice, an area of study, or a profession. We had not even established OD as a theory or even as a practice.

We decided that there was a need for something that would describe the state of OD. Our intention was to each write a book and also to recruit three other authors. After some searching, we found a young editor who had just joined the small publishing house of Addison-Wesley. We made contact, and the series was born. Our audience was to be human resource professionals who spent their time consulting with managers in their development through various small-group activities, such as team building. More than thirty books have been published in that series, and the series has had a life of its own. We just celebrated its thirtieth anniversary.

At last year's National OD Network Conference, I said that it was time for the OD profession to change and transform itself. Is that not what we change agents tell our clients to do? This new Jossey-Bass/Pfeiffer series will do just that. It can be seen as:

- A documentation of the re-invention of OD;

- An effort that will take us to the next level; and

- A practical effort to transfer to the world the theory and practice of leading-edge practitioners and theorists.

The books in this new series will thus prove to be valuable resources for change agents to keep current with the new and leading-edge ideas and practices.

May this very exciting change agent series be most creative and innovative. May it give our field a renewed burst of energy and awareness.

Richard Beckhard
Written on Labor Day weekend 1999 from my summer cabin near Bethel, Maine

About the Editors

William J. Rothwell, Ph.D.,** is president of Rothwell and Associates, a private consulting firm, as well as professor of human resources development on the University Park Campus of The Pennsylvania State University. Before arriving at Penn State in 1993, he was an assistant vice president and management development director for a major insurance company and a training director in a state government agency. He has worked full-time in human resources management and employee training and development from 1979 to the present. He thus combines real-world experience with academic and consulting experience. As a consultant, Dr. Rothwell's client list includes over thirty-five companies from the Fortune 500.

Dr. Rothwell received his Ph.D. with a specialization in employee training from the University of Illinois at Urbana-Champaign, his M.B.A. with a specialization in human resources management from Sangamon State University (now called the

University of Illinois at Springfield), his M.A. from the University of Illinois at Urbana-Champaign, and his B.A. from Illinois State University. He holds lifetime accreditation as a Senior Professional in Human Resources (SPHR), has been accredited as a Registered Organization Development Consultant (RODC), and holds the industry designation as Fellow of the Life Management Institute (FLMI).

Dr. Rothwell's latest publications include *The Manager and Change Leader* (ASTD, 2001); *The Role of Intervention Selector, Designer and Developer, and Implementor* (ASTD, 2000); *ASTD Models for Human Performance* (2nd ed.) (ASTD, 2000); *The Analyst* (ASTD, 2000); *The Evaluator* (ASTD, 2000); *The ASTD Reference Guide to Workplace Learning and Performance* (3rd ed.), with H. Sredl (HRD Press, 2000); *The Complete Guide to Training Delivery: A Competency-Based Approach,* with S. King and M. King (AMACOM, 2000); *Human Performance Improvement: Building Practitioner Competence,* with C. Hohne and S. King (Butterworth-Heinemann, 2000); *Effective Succession Planning: Ensuring Leadership Continuity and Building Talent from Within* (2nd ed.) (AMACOM, 2000); and *The Competency Toolkit,* with D. Dubois (HRD Press, 2000).

Roland Sullivan, RODC, has worked as an OD pioneer with nearly eight hundred systems in eleven countries and virtually every major industry. Richard Beckhard has recognized him as one of the world's first one hundred change agents.

Mr. Sullivan specializes in the science and art of systematic and systemic change, executive team building, and facilitating Whole System Transformation Conferences—large interactive meetings with 300 to 1,500 people. Over 25,000 people have participated in his conferences worldwide; one co-facilitated with Kristine Quade held for the Amalgamated Bank of South Africa was named runner-up for the title of outstanding change project of the world by the OD Institute.

With William Rothwell and Gary McLean, he is revising one of the field's seminal books, *Practicing OD: A Consultant's Guide* (Jossey-Bass/Pfeiffer, 1995). The first edition is now translated into Chinese.

He did his graduate work in organization development at Pepperdine University and Loyola University.

Mr. Sullivan's current interests include the following: Whole-system transformation, balancing economic and human realities; discovering and collaborating with cutting-edge change-focused authors who are documenting the perpetual renewal of the OD profession; and applied phenomenology: developing higher states of consciousness and self-awareness in the consulting of interdependent organizations.

Mr. Sullivan's current professional learning is available at www.rolandsullivan.com.

Kristine **Quade** is an independent consultant who combines her background as an attorney with a master's degree in organization development from Pepperdine University and years of experience as both an internal and external OD consultant.

Ms. Quade draws from experiences in guiding teams from divergent areas within corporations and across many levels of executives and employees. She has facilitated leadership alignment, culture change, support system alignment, quality process improvements, organizational redesign, and the creation of clear strategic intent that results in significant bottom-line results. A believer in whole-system change, she has developed the expertise to facilitate groups ranging in size from eight to two thousand in the same room for a three-day change process.

Recognized as the 1996 Minnesota Organization Development Practitioner of the Year, Ms. Quade teaches in the master's programs at Pepperdine University and the University of Minnesota at Mankato and the master's and doctoral programs at the University of St. Thomas in Minneapolis. She is a frequent presenter at the Organization Development National Conference and also at the International OD Congress and the International Association of Facilitators.

About the Authors

Jacqueline Byrd, Ph.D., is president of the Richard Byrd Company, a forty-year-old Minneapolis-based management consulting firm that serves both national and international clients. Dr. Byrd assists organizations in:

- The design and management of complex system change initiatives;

- Succession planning and leadership coaching and development; and

- Strategic planning designed to position for future organizational success.

She is also the brain behind *Creatrix* (www.creatrix.com), designed to build the innovative capacity of individuals, teams, and organizations. Some of Dr. Byrd's clients include Alliant Techsystems, Cargill, Caterpillar Paving Products, Ecolab, HealthPartners & Regions Hospital, Pentair, Toro Company, 3M, the City of Minneapolis, and the University of Minnesota.

Dr. Byrd is serving as adjunct faculty in the University of St. Thomas' Organizational Development Program. She is a graduate of the University of Minnesota and has extensive training in organization change and leadership development.

As an author and speaker, she has published and addressed the subjects of innovation, creativity, risk taking, leadership, coaching, and strategies for implementing change. She is a member of the National OD Network, and the American Society for Training and Development (ASTD).

Paul Lockwood Brown, MBA, has been with the Creatrix team, an innovation of the Richard Byrd Company, since its inception. He joined the firm as a consultant, bringing with him a rich and diverse history in management and leadership positions. He has held progressively more responsible leadership positions in manufacturing, service, and retail industries and has served in the United States Air Force. His broad depth of knowledge in applied leadership principles has propelled his success throughout his career.

Mr. Brown earned his MBA from the University of St. Thomas, St. Paul, Minnesota, after completing his undergraduate work in organizational behavior and communications at Concordia University, St. Paul, Minnesota, where he graduated summa cum laude. He is currently pursuing his doctorate at the University of St. Thomas in organization development and learning.

Mr. Brown has held positions on various boards throughout his career. He has been a director at the Greater Minneapolis Area Chapter of the American Red Cross, where he has held the office of treasurer. He is also an adjunct faculty member at Concordia University, St. Paul, teaching at both the graduate and undergraduate levels.

He is a member of the Minnesota OD Network, the National OD Network, the American Management Association, and the American Society for Training and Development (ASTD).

Index